DREAM HUSTLE INSPIRE

A CULTURE SHIFT IMPRINT

A RELLY RELL STUDIOS COMPANY

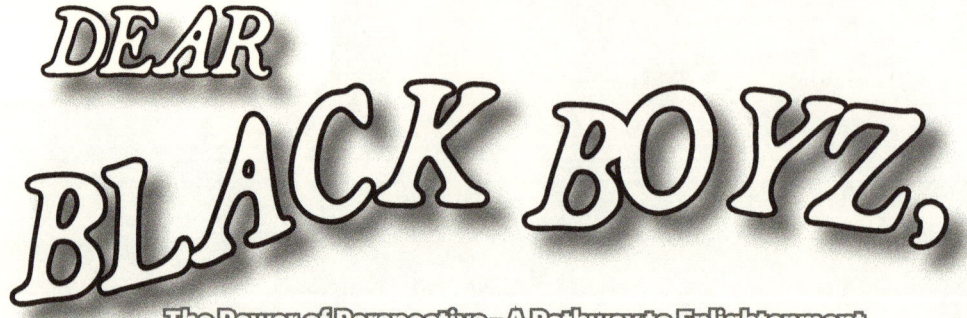

DEAR BLACK BOYZ,
The Power of Perspective - A Pathway to Enlightenment

PUBLISHED BY
DREAM HUSTLE INSPIRE, A CULTURE SHIFT IMPRINT

AUTHOR: RELLY RELL

Book Design and Illustrations: Relly Rell

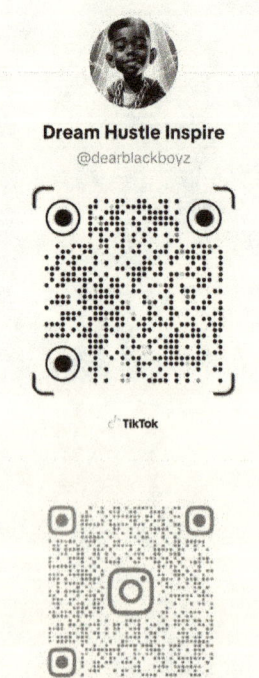

PUBLISHED BY DREAM HUSTLE INSPIRE,

A CULTURE SHIFT IMPRINT

Copyright ©2024 Relly Rell

This edition first published in 2024
by
22 Freedom Path, Empowerment City, DHI 11144

www.RellyRellStudios.com

www.DearBlackBoyz.com

All rights reserved. This publication may not be reproduced, stored or transmitted in any form or by any means without prior permission of the publisher. Culture Shift Imprint published in the USA in 2024. Printed and bound in the USA by Dream Hustle Inspire, LLC.

The author of this book does not dispense medical advice or prescribe the use of any technique as a form of treatment for physical, emotional or medical problems without the advice of a physician, either directly or indirectly. The intent of the author is only to offer information of a general nature to help you in your quest for emotional, physical, and spiritual well-being. In the event you use any of the information in this book for yourself, the author and the publisher assume no responsibility for your actions.

Edited by Shifu Dr. Tim Thompson & Matthew Allinson

Book Design by Relly Rell

Keeven Jack, Culture Shifter and Influencer

Paperback ISBN 979-8-9889156-0-7

WHO ARE YOU?

| I AM! |

TABLE OF CONTENTS

DEDICATION	I	PEACE	24
LA TIMES ARTICLE	II-III	THE PURPOSE OF LOVE	31
DEAR BLACK Boyz,	IV-V	COMMUNICATION	32
STANDING IN YOUR GREATNESS	VI	UNDERSTANDING A WOMAN'S PERSPECTIVE	35
FOREWORD BY THE UNIVERSE	VII	SELFLESS	40
INSPIRE YOUR HIGHEST SELF	VIII	EMOTIONS	41
INTRODUCTION	IX	THE POWER OF PERSPECTIVE	42
THE POWER OF PERSPECTIVE	XII	HEAVEN HERE ON EARTH	43
INFORMATION IS HIDDEN WITHIN THESE BOOKS	XIV	FINAL LETTER TO BLACK BOYZ	48
		WAKE UP!!!	50
DREAMZZZ	XV	BLACK BOYZ ALPHABET	51-52
CONFIDENCE	1	BLACK BOYZ AFFIRMATIONS	53
STORY ONE	2	BLACK BOYZ CODE OF CONDUCT	53
STORY TWO	4	THE SECRET TO LIFE	54
STORY THREE	7	COMPLETION	55
RISE ABOVE THE HUSTLE	15	ABOUT THE AUTHOR	56
ENERGY	16	BREAKING THE CHAIN GAME	58-59
NEGATIVE ENERGY	18	THE KEY	60
POSITIVE ENERGY	22	MIRROR MIRROR MIRROR	63

DEDICATION

This book is the light for the wandering souls of Black Boyz who are on the path of self-discovery. It's especially dedicated to those in search of their highest essence, yearning for awakening and the purest form of self-love. More specifically, this book is for you—standing at the brink of enlightenment, ready to embrace your true, divine nature.

"Dear Black Boyz" embodies a mindset that keeps building on its own upward momentum as we embrace "The Power of Perspective." This transformative perspective is the key to shifting our consciousness, illuminating a path toward self-realization and empowerment.

Within these pages, you'll find a profound exploration of the contrasts between Religion, Spirituality, and Consciousness. This book serves as a guide for you to awaken your highest self, to break free from the cycles that have bound us all, and to step into your full power as a Black Boy.

Remember, you're not just a Boy navigating life—you're first and foremost a manifestation of the divine, experiencing this journey as a Black Boy by choice. This world may have its limitations, but your true worth is infinite. You hold the power to shape your destiny and the destiny of generations to come.

Pictured from left to right are Terrell White (Relly Rell), Tony Walker, and Tyrone White.

Los Angeles Times

ARTICLE BY STEVE HENSON, OCT. 31, 1996

Antelope Valley's Walker has Division I talent but likely will attend junior college because of a learning disability.

This LA Times article about my brother painted a misleading picture, suggesting that he faced learning challenges, but it failed to acknowledge the truth—my brother never had a learning disability. The California public school system has long disabled and neglected Black Boyz like us, stifling their potential despite them possessing D1 talent. This article should have said, "A system that failed to nurture true potential!"

Picture of Tony Walker at Utah State University.

Los Angeles Times

WALKER HEADED FOR UTAH STATE, APR. 4, 1997

Walker, an all-purpose back, was considered the best player in the state of California nobody could recruit.

Tony Walker isn't just my big brother; he has always been my hero and a living example of resilience. Even back in 1996, he was showing me what it means to rise above challenges and never let the world define you. Tony's journey back then taught me that our greatest strength lies within us, in our ability to tap into our true purpose and power. He was, and still is, proof that no matter how tough the odds, we have the power to create our own destiny.

Through Tony, I learned—and continue to learn—that as Black Boyz, we carry a power that the world often fears. But instead of letting that fear hold us back, we must embrace it, own it, and let it fuel our journey. Tony unknowingly reminds me that everything we need is already inside us—we just need to remember. Even now, he continues to show me that amazing truth through his actions and presence.

His life, even as far back as 1996, has been a testament to the strength and potential within all of us, and I want every Black Boy to know they have that same power to rise and walk in their own light.

III | **Dear Black Boyz,**

DEAR BLACK BOYZ,

The world may try to define you with misconceptions and stereotypes, but I see you for who you truly are. You're not what the world says—YOU ARE a God on a human journey, experiencing life as a Black Boy by intention. We chose this path, and with it, we face challenges and harness strengths unique to us.

It's not always easy to grasp the purpose behind our existence. Life's cycles will continue until we awaken to our true selves. So, I call on you, Black Boy, to awaken. Discover the truth of who you are. Will you be the one to break these cycles, or will you allow them to continue stunting your growth and blocking the fulfillment of your awesome potential?

Our history is one of resilience in the face of adversity. The world hasn't been fair to Black Boyz, but our ancestors showed us how to endure and thrive. We're just four generations away from slavery, three from segregation, two from the crack epidemic, and one from mass incarceration. Despite these obstacles, we rise. The world may attempt to hold us down, but remember, those destined to lead will always find a way.

We, the Black Boyz, are destined to overcome. We will rise above every challenge this generation presents. So embrace who you truly are, for there's great power in being a Black Boy. By opening yourself to different perspectives, you gain the freedom to live life on your own terms. You become the author of your own story, crafting a narrative of strength, peace, and fulfillment.

Never allow the world to define you. You are powerful, you are loved, and you are confidently and proudly Black. The time has come to awaken to your greatness. The time has come to take charge of your destiny and shape it into the vision you see for yourself.

-Relly Rell

DEAR BLACK BOYZ,

Young and curious, in a White man's world, breaking you down brick by brick.

Trying to kill you and control you, because your roots are thick.

When they try to tell you how to act.

"You're Ghetto," "You're Different," or "You don't act Black."

Remember, you are Powerful, Loved, Confident, and Proudly Black.

-Ja Kobi Cockerham

Standing In Your Greatness
by Relly Rell

Dear Black Boyz,

FOREWORD BY THE UNIVERSE

To the Black Boyz of Today, Tomorrow, and Eternity,

I AM the Universe, the boundless expanse of energy that surrounds, connects, and sustains all things. I have witnessed the birth of stars, the rise of civilizations, and the endless cycles of creation and transformation. But today, I turn my gaze toward you, the Black Boyz who stand on the precipice of your own greatness. You may not always see it, but you are woven from the very fabric of my being—crafted from stardust, endowed with the power to shape reality, and destined to illuminate the world with your unique brilliance. In these pages, you will find the whispers of ancient truths and the echoes of future possibilities, all converging in the present moment to guide you on your path.

This book, *Dear Black Boyz,: The Power of Perspective - A Pathway to Enlightenment*, is a gift from me to you. It is a reminder that within you lies the same force that fuels the sun, that turns the tides, that drives the winds. It is a testament to your inherent strength, your boundless energy, your unshakable confidence, and your profound emotions—all tools for crafting the life you are meant to live. As you journey through this book, remember that you are not alone. You are connected to the vast network of existence—each breath you take is a conversation with the cosmos, each heartbeat a rhythm in the eternal symphony. Your confidence is the spark that ignites change; your energy is the current that powers your dreams; your communication is the bridge that connects souls; and your emotions are the waves that carry you toward your destiny.

Understand this: You are both the creator and the creation. The thoughts you nurture, the actions you take, the words you speak—they all resonate across the fabric of reality, shaping the world in ways both seen and unseen. Master your energy, and you will master your destiny. Cultivate your confidence, and you will inspire others to rise. Honor your emotions, and you will navigate life's currents with grace and wisdom. The path ahead is yours to walk, but know that with each step, I am with you. I am the ground beneath your feet, the wind at your back, the stars that light your way. I am the potential within you, the dreams that stir in your soul, the whisper of possibility in your ear.

As you embark on this journey, remember that greatness is not a destination but a state of being. It is the realization of your true self, the manifestation of your deepest purpose. You are not just a Boy—you are a universe in motion, a constellation of possibilities, a beacon of light in a world that needs your brilliance. So step forward, Black Boyz, with your heads held high and your spirits unwavering. Embrace the power of your perspective, for it is through this lens that you will transform the world. Know that you are loved, that you are powerful, that you are infinite. This is your time. This is your path. This is your universe.

With infinite love and boundless possibilities,
-The Universe

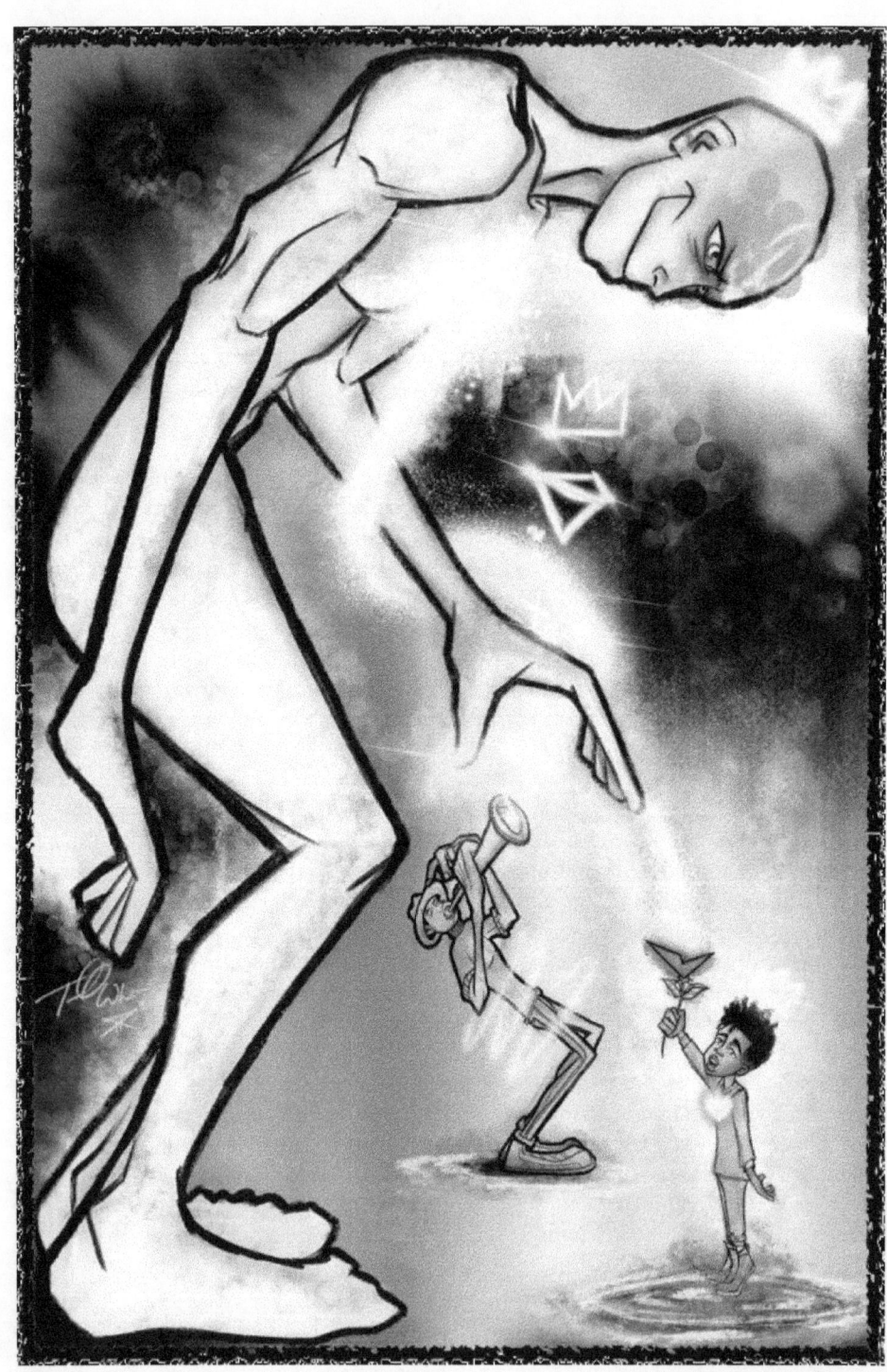

Inspire Your Highest Self
by Relly Rell

Dear Black Boyz,

INTRODUCTION

I'll be honest—reading has never been something I enjoyed. The idea of sitting down with a book was, and still is, unappealing to me. But let me explain why.

My siblings and I grew up in Lancaster, California, a place we called "The Land." Back in the late nineties and early 2000s, we thought we'd never leave. Now, as adults with our own children, "The Land" is just a memory, a place we left behind because it trapped us in a cycle of negativity that gradually eroded the positivity we once had.

If you know anything about California's public schools, especially for Boyz of color, you understand the impact of gang culture and subpar education. Schools in Black communities often have lower standards, staffed by less qualified teachers. Sadly, we've come to accept this as normal, believing that we don't deserve better. It's heartbreaking to see how low the quality of education is in our neighborhoods, and even more distressing that so many of us are grateful for the little we receive.

Most Black families, isolated from white communities, remain unaware of the better options available for their children. I've seen this disparity firsthand, raising my kids in predominantly white states like Utah and Colorado. Even the worst schools there are better than the best schools in the neighborhoods where I grew up.

Growing up in California, it was clear that our neighborhoods were forgotten by the so-called educational system. Our struggles were romanticized, not addressed. It's tough to accept the disadvantages Black kids face in the public school system—always several steps behind our peers, our opportunities limited, negative stereotypes reinforced.

I've witnessed the damage done by the lack of resources in marginalized communities and how it erodes hope, especially for young Black Boyz. Career opportunities are limited if sports aren't your thing, and the broken education system keeps us trapped, fighting for the scraps left by others. We talk about the "Trap" in reference to the drug houses, but the real trap is the community itself, a system designed to make us believe we're destined to fail or accept less because of our skin color. We're constantly indoctrinated, either imprisoned by self-limiting beliefs or pushed to break free from them. But self-education, a potential escape from the neighborhood and the broken system, was never encouraged. Thinking for ourselves and questioning the status quo was not part of the plan.

In communities like ours, success is often portrayed through television, limited to careers in sports, music, and entertainment. The streets and gang life never counted to me because they only led to two outcomes: jail or death. That was never what I wanted to associate with as a path to success.

In our home, the only book was the Bible. Its complex language didn't match the way we spoke, making it an unlikely choice for casual reading. My siblings and I struggled with literacy, a problem made worse by the failing public school system. Teachers rarely helped, and without support at home, insecurity and low self-esteem took root.

In school, I faced ridicule and mockery, which crushed my self-esteem. I hid behind a persona named "Excuses" to cope with the shame. It provided temporary relief, but the fear always resurfaced when I was called to read aloud. The public school system, as I experienced it, was designed to kill curiosity and stifle independent thinking. Any deviation from their curriculum was met with severe consequences. The system erased our rich cultural heritage, ignored our ancestors' contributions, and promoted a narrative of white supremacy. We were taught to accept this as normal, oblivious to the fact that we're integral stakeholders in society, descendants of those who built it.

Growing up in a single-parent household, my brothers and I moved around a lot, attending eleven schools in twelve years. This instability created a sense of inferiority in me, leading me to blame others for not helping me overcome my struggles. I almost fell for their manipulation, nearly letting them strip away my creativity and free thinking. I began to believe I wasn't capable of thriving in "The Land," and these excuses chipped away at my self-confidence. I started identifying with my insecurities, accepting them as my fate, feeling trapped in a system with no escape.

Historically, the public school system has failed Black Boyz, especially since integration in 1954. Like many before me, I was almost swallowed by this broken system that neglects Black children. The only way to fix it is for parents to become proactive in their children's education and push for changes. Passive acceptance will not prioritize our needs. We must ignite change from within, understanding that it's essential for progress.

There's nothing more powerful than a Black Man who thinks for himself, who is purposeful and self-reliant. Society fears this, so they try to contain us within the constraints of a metaphorical prison cell and the public education system. If educators lack the motivation or capability to teach critical thinking, then it's up to us to foster this skill within ourselves and challenge the system.

For years, I used my dislike of reading as a crutch. I always had an excuse. During my time in public school, I never had a Black teacher. Was this by design, part of a larger systemic plan? Or did the system drive Black teachers away? As a kid, these seemed like real possibilities. But as I grew older, I realized the truth—everything was a façade. The police, the schools, the hospitals—they were all illusions, designed to make us feel less than, to trap us in fear and excuses, convincing us there was no escape from "The Trap." Sports and art saved me from this societal box. Drawing, a natural talent, became my escape. It allowed me to explore my creativity and think for myself. I used art to face my fears and failures, and I learned I wasn't bound by society's constraints. I found a loophole. Art gave me a safe space to make mistakes, unlike the cruelty I was experiencing from the judgmental world around me. Mistakes became symbols of growth and positivity.

My intense focus on art transformed me. It not only improved my skills quickly but also transitioned me from a target of ridicule to someone who was praised. I even started selling my art, boosting my confidence further. Through art, I found my voice, and for the first time, I felt heard.

Discovering my artistic abilities made me an entrepreneur at a young age. I offered my art services to classmates, making me unique and financially independent. Art helped me escape the restrictive education system and think freely. It helped me regain confidence and illuminated the path to self- discovery.
Reading was never interesting to me because the school books didn't represent Black voices. It wasn't until later that I found books that connected with my experiences and taught me valuable life lessons. This showed me the importance of Critical Race Theory (CRT) and self-discovery. Reading plays a crucial role in leading a fulfilling life. It gives us the power to break free from societal limitations and enhances our creativity and vocabulary.

Instead of blaming others or making excuses, I've chosen to start where I am and create my own path. I've faced my fears, taught myself to read, and changed my perspective. I no longer see "The Trap" as a dead end but as a stepping stone. With art as my guide, I created a new belief system that allowed me to imagine a future only I could create. It's empowering to make your own way, without competition.

Overcoming my fear of reading unlocked my creativity and set me on a path toward health, wealth, success, and peace of mind. As the author of my own story, I'm constantly improving my reading skills. While reading still isn't my favorite thing, I'm no longer struggling with illiteracy. Reading is essential for young Black Boyz because it lays the foundation for survival and success. It can take you further than sports or music ever could. A love for reading creates lifelong habits that can be passed down through generations. It offers a new perspective that can grow into greatness.

If reading isn't your thing or if you struggle with it, I challenge you to practice daily. You might start to enjoy it. If not, write your own story and read it. Don't be disheartened by spelling mistakes; today's technology takes away all excuses. Reading is powerful—it can transport you to worlds you never imagined, open doors you never knew existed, and turn dreams into reality. Your words are your genie: speak them into existence, and watch them manifest.

This journey isn't just about surviving—it's about thriving, rising above every obstacle, and claiming the greatness that is your birthright. Remember, Black Boy, the world is waiting for your story. Don't just read the words on the page—live them. Let them guide you, empower you, and lead you to a future where you define your destiny.

The Power of Perspective

In writing this book, my purpose is to guide you through life's challenges by offering you a new lens through which to view the world. The simple question, "What if ?" forms the foundation of this work. I'm not here to impose morality or tell you what's right or wrong. Instead, I'm inviting you to explore a different perspective—one that could spark change and lead you to a better version of yourself.

Our beliefs are deeply rooted in our personal experiences, making it difficult for anyone to alter them. Think about a time when you were firm in your viewpoint, and someone tried to change your mind. Most likely, their efforts were in vain unless you had a moment of clarity that shifted your perspective.

To embrace a new perspective, you must be willing to let go of your current one. An open mind is essential for self-improvement, and books, when read with an open heart, can be a powerful catalyst for this change. This book aims to be that catalyst. But before we continue, I want to ask you a simple question that'll test your openness to new ideas: Can you see things from the Devil's perspective?

Now, I know what you're probably thinking. The mere mention of the Devil might evoke feelings of fear or unease. But rest assured, this isn't about devil worship or selling your soul. The question is designed to challenge your understanding of perspective. In many cultures, the Devil represents pure evil, an absolute negative. But what if you could turn that negative into a positive? What if you could see things from a completely different viewpoint?

If you're still with me, let's explore this theory further. Imagine a world where everything you thought you knew was turned upside down. What if the truths you were taught are flawed? What if the Devil and God are not so different after all? What if the stories we've been told are incomplete or even manipulated? Does this shift your thinking? Does it make you more curious? Curiosity, after all, is the catalyst for change.

When I ask "What if?" I'm not seeking to determine what's right or wrong. I'm challenging you to question everything, to open your mind to new possibilities, new realities, and new truths. This isn't about fear; it's about wonder. A fresh perspective can captivate you, just as it has the potential to transform your life. As you encounter new perspectives, I encourage you to embrace them with an open mind. Give them a fair chance to turn bad into good. Just as you, a young Black Boy, deserve a fair opportunity to be seen for who you truly are—a valuable member of society, not the negative stereotypes that have been imposed on us.

The "Devil's Perspective" is nothing more than a prompt for personal growth. Understanding it can equip you with a powerful tool to apply in your life, creating clarity and improving outcomes. My purpose in writing this book is to share the wisdom I've gained, hoping that it reaches you at a much earlier stage in your life than it did for me.

As a Black Boy growing up in California, I've witnessed many unsettling things on the streets. I understand the fears we grapple with daily. My mission is to help free all Black Boyz from the mindset that enslaves us. No matter your race, there is something in this book for everyone. But I can only share my experiences as a Black Man who has evolved into a profound thinker.

Each of us has our own unique narrative. This is mine. I share it in the hope that it'll inspire those who can relate to my journey. The wisdom in this book comes from a shift in my own life perspective. A change in perspective allows you to see life through a different prism, turning negatives into positives. For example, embracing a perspective of self-love brings inner peace. The Power of Perspective is not just about personal transformation; it's about breaking generational curses and laying the groundwork for a new cultural practice—one that frees us from the harmful habits that have kept us bound.

I dedicate this book to all my Black Boyz, for your purpose is the driving force that keeps you moving forward, even when the road is tough. This book is meant to help you flip any negative situation in your life into a positive one. All it takes is asking yourself one simple question: What if?

Information Is Hidden Within These Books
by Relly Rell

XIV | **Dear Black Boyz,**

Dreamzzz
by Relly Rell

XV | Dear Black Boyz,

CHAPTER ONE
CONFIDENCE

A Boy who never finds confidence in himself will grow into a man who struggles to find his purpose. For young Black Boyz, nurturing confidence is essential to discovering inner peace and understanding their mission in life. Confidence lays the foundation for everything we do. It gives us the ability to believe in ourselves, trust our intuition, and develop the courage to think independently.

However, confidence can be fragile. My experiences with sports have shown me that they can be both a powerful builder and a swift destroyer of confidence. Sports can rapidly boost your self-assurance, but they can also quickly tear it down.

To explore the concept of confidence, I will share three stories—stories that I've lived, witnessed, and experienced from my own perspective—each highlighting the delicate balance of confidence in the world of sports.

Story One
The Dunk

My older brother, Tony Walker, was my hero growing up. To me, Tony was like a Black Superhero when it came to sports. He was dominant in both football and basketball, excelling in ways that left me in awe. Tony was an ESPN Top 25 Defensive Back in football, recruited by top colleges across the country in the 90s. But due to issues with the public school system and a lack of resources and guidance, he ended up at Utah State University. The broken public school system that so many of us fall victim to played a significant role in that outcome.

Tony was the best undersized athlete I've ever seen—he reminded me of Allen Iverson, but if Iverson had chosen football over basketball. I vividly remember Tony dunking on a 12-foot rim when he was in the 10th grade at the elementary school across the street from our duplex. The school had raised the rims to 12 feet to prevent them from being broken or stolen by kids hanging on them, but that didn't stop Tony. He dunked on those rims just to prove a point, showcasing his athletic prowess and leaving everyone in awe.

Despite what you might think, Tony wasn't 6'9" like LeBron James—he was just six feet tall. But he performed these incredible feats as if he were a giant. Watching him do these things left a lasting impression on me, a sixth-grader at the time, dreaming of what I could achieve. Seeing Tony, I believed that I could follow in his footsteps, that I was cut from the same cloth.

I was good at football, but I realized early on that I didn't like getting hit in the cold. The contact wasn't the issue—it was the freezing temperatures that made it unbearable for me. So, I gravitated toward basketball, determined to prove that I could be better than my brother, the superhero. I set my goals high, always striving to surpass Tony, and that competition became my driving force. I had an unwavering confidence in myself, a belief that nothing could stop me.

By the time I was in the 8th grade, I was already better than anyone in my age bracket. I spent every day playing against Tony, developing a killer instinct that made me fearless on the court. If I could hold my own against him, I knew I could play with anyone. Tony never took it easy on me—every basket I scored against him was earned.

In 9th grade, I dominated all the other freshmen, and by my sophomore year, I was the starting point guard at the same high school where Tony was a legend. It was like trying to fill Michael Jordan's shoes, but I welcomed the challenge. I was determined to surpass everyone's expectations and make a name for myself. Starting on varsity as a sophomore was something Tony had never accomplished, and I knew then that I was on track to surpass him in basketball.

But I was still a small, skinny kid, standing at 5'9" and barely able to touch the rim. That's when I set a new goal for myself: to be like Allen Iverson. Iverson was every basketball player's hero in the late 1990s and early 2000s, especially for those of us under six feet tall. His confidence, his ability to dominate the game despite his size—that's what I aspired to. I modeled everything I did after Iverson, from my game on the court to wearing his signature shoes throughout high school.

The only thing holding me back was my inability to dunk. Iverson was dunking on seven-footers, and I could barely touch the rim. But I knew that if I could dunk, I would be unstoppable. The summer after my sophomore year, I set a single goal: to dunk before the next basketball season. I believed, without a doubt, that I would go from touching the rim to dunking on seven-footers, just like Iverson, in four months.

Looking back, it was a lofty goal, but I was driven. For four straight months, I pushed myself to the limit, doing 1,000 calf raises and jump roping with strength shoes every day. I took no days off, dedicated to the process and believing that I would achieve my goal. I didn't even attempt a single dunk until the first open gym for tryouts four months later. My goal was to dunk with ease, and I was willing to push myself as hard as possible to make it happen.

When tryouts came, I was ready. The gym was packed with about 50 high school kids, all waiting for tryouts to start. I was telling my teammate, Steve Wilkinson, that I could dunk now, even though I hadn't tried it yet. Steve, who was 6'5" and could dunk, didn't believe me, but I was confident. I told him I could do a reverse rock-the-cradle dunk with two hands—a dunk I had never tried before in my life.

With everyone watching, I dribbled up to the baseline, jumped off one foot, and completed the dunk with ease. The gym exploded. Steve was the most excited of them all, running around and telling everyone what he had just witnessed. The other players, especially my teammate Eric Williams, couldn't believe it. Eric, who could jump out of the gym but could never complete a dunk, was the main one doubting me.

But I didn't care. My confidence was through the roof, and I knew I could do it again. So, with everyone watching, I went back to the baseline, dribbled up, and dunked again, just as easily as the first time. The gym went wild. I had put in the work over the summer, and now I was seeing the results.

After that, I started dunking all the time in practice, and my confidence kept growing. I felt unstoppable. All the hard work I'd put in became the blueprint for everything I did when it came to achieving my goals. When my older brother Tony came to one of my games during my senior year in Utah, I knew it was my time to show him what I could do. I had 29 points and three dunks in that game, and seeing the pride in Tony's eyes made all the sacrifices worth it.

This story is an example of how you can build confidence in yourself. I found something I loved, set high standards, and worked tirelessly to surpass them. Confidence is crucial for every Black Boy— without it, you become fearful, and fear makes you a slave to other people's perspectives. But with confidence, you can achieve anything you set your mind to. My journey from a small, skinny kid who could barely touch the rim to a confident player who could dunk with ease is proof of that.

Story Two
Facing Fear

My wife and I are blessed with an exceptional young man, our son, Ja Kobi. He's smart, funny, good-looking, and has the athletic build of a top high school football player. Freshman year arrived, and after much anticipation, his mother finally allowed him to play football. From the moment he got the green light, Ja Kobi was all in—his excitement was palpable. He said all the right things, brimming with self-confidence, and together, we trained hard every day. I pushed him as I pushed myself when striving for improvement, instilling in him the importance of hard work, discipline, and mastering the fundamentals.

As summer football camp approached, Ja Kobi was ready to prove himself. Camp was more about conditioning, team bonding, and getting to know the coaches than full-contact drills. But even without the helmet and pads, Ja Kobi carried himself with an air of confidence. He made the team, earning starting positions as a middle linebacker on defense and a fullback on offense. Despite facing a steep learning curve with this being his first year playing football, I was confident that with commitment, he would overcome it. I had already set the expectation that practicing with me would be harder than anything he'd face from his coaches.

Hard work and consistency were our guiding principles. Mastering the fundamentals, I told him, was the fastest route to confidence. Without that diligence and consistency, confidence quickly turns into hollow boasting. True confidence comes from putting in the work, day in and day out. But all that changed when the helmet and pads came out.

The first time Ja Kobi got hit hard was in a scrimmage against a local team. A massive 6'4" running back charged at him full speed, and in that split second, all the training and confidence drained from Ja Kobi's body. He didn't believe he could make the tackle, and that doubt was all it took. The impact knocked him back five yards, leaving him flat on his back as the running back scored a touchdown. I watched as the confidence got knocked out of him along with the wind.

From that moment on, fear began to creep into Ja Kobi's game. With each passing game, he grew more hesitant to hit anyone bigger than him, even if they were just a bit taller. My wife and I noticed how he started making excuses—blaming his teammates, the coaches, anything to deflect from his own performance. My wife, never one to let things slide, demanded that his results match his talk.

My approach was different; I believed in taking away all his excuses by putting in the work. We drilled and practiced every day until there was no room for excuses, leaving only the need to prove himself.

By Game 7, Ja Kobi was presented with the perfect opportunity to do just that. On a kickoff return, he had a clear shot at the opposing player. This kid was a little taller than Ja Kobi but not nearly as physically imposing. As they closed in on each other, Ja Kobi hesitated, and that was all it took. The opposing player knocked him off balance, injuring Ja Kobi's leg and putting him out for the rest of the game. My wife was furious—she knew he'd missed his chance to believe in himself, to conquer his fear.

The car ride home was tense. My wife lit into him, frustrated that he was lying to himself about his confidence. She told him in no uncertain terms that if he didn't confront his fears, his football days would be over by the end of the season. This was the first step toward accountability, and she made it clear that accountability was essential for growth. Accountability, I explained to Ja Kobi, is a two-step process. The first step is surrounding yourself with people who care enough to be honest with you and hold you accountable. The second, and most challenging step, is being brutally honest with yourself and holding yourself accountable for your own progress. We could hold Ja Kobi accountable all day, but it wouldn't matter if he didn't hold himself accountable.

To face his fear head-on, Ja Kobi decided to challenge me to a one-on-one hitting match. Let me put this in perspective: I'm 6'2", 195 pounds, and Ja Kobi, at the time, was 5'6", 160 pounds. For him to want to go up against me was an act of bravery in itself. I knew this was his way of trying to overcome his fear, so I went online and ordered shoulder pads to make sure we were both protected. There would be no excuses.

The evening came, and I told Ja Kobi to suit up. I could sense the fear building in him as I emerged from the room, decked out in all Black—new shoulder pads, a Black jersey, the works. I knew the sight alone would strike fear into him, and that was the point. His mind was already working against him, filling with doubt before we even lined up. But despite his fear, he stood tall, ready to face the challenge.

We lined up five yards apart for a simple collision drill. I made him decide when to start, ensuring that this was his choice, not mine. We stood there for what felt like an eternity—five minutes of intense emotion and fear on Ja Kobi's part. I could see the battle going on inside him, but I knew I couldn't help him. He had to overcome this on his own. Finally, he shouted, "GO!"

I exploded out of my stance like a madman, closing the gap between us in an instant. Ja Kobi's fear froze him in place, and I hit him hard. The impact was fierce, and while he didn't fall, I knew he felt every bit of it. Tears streamed down his face—he'd been defeated by his own fear before the drill even began.

In that moment, I knew it was time to teach him about the second stage of accountability. I explained that fear is a product of the mind, created by negative thoughts. The pain he felt was temporary, lasting only a few seconds, but his fear made it feel like a lifetime. He had to understand that the pain wasn't because of my size—it was because he froze and didn't use the proper technique. If he wanted to succeed, he had to confront that fear and hold himself accountable.

I pushed him to try again, this time with the proper technique and mindset. It wasn't easy—he was still scared, still fighting the doubt that had taken root in his mind. But after countless rounds, something shifted. His mindset changed, and he began to fight back. The fear that had paralyzed him was being replaced by a newfound confidence. When survival becomes the only option, confidence reaches its peak.

We went at it over 100 times until all of Ja Kobi's fears were gone. I watched as his negative mindset transformed into a positive one, allowing him to hold himself accountable. I believe that this newfound confidence will take him far in his football career. His limitations are only a product of his mentality, and when he told me he wanted to be the next Aaron Donald, I believed him.

In the end, the lesson for Ja Kobi—and for anyone reading this—is simple: don't let your fears keep you from your dreams. Self-accountability is the key to true and lasting growth. When you can look within, face your fears, and take responsibility for your progress, there's nothing you can't achieve. What do you believe you deserve? Whatever it is, know that you can achieve it, because greatness is inherent in you as a child of God.

Story Three
Fear, Emotion, and the Moment

The final story I'll share revolves around the influential figures in our lives that can either fortify or undermine our self-belief. As a coach for a 2nd and 3rd grade basketball team at the YMCA, I witnessed firsthand how families, especially parents, project their fears and expectations onto their children. I saw how rapidly a child's confidence can teeter between positive and negative. This tale might help you recognize those individuals in your life who've imposed their own fears and expectations upon you, causing self-doubt. The key isn't why this deep-seated self-doubt occasionally surfaces; what matters is the expectations we set for ourselves. Unfortunately, the fears and expectations of others can cripple your self-assuredness, with lingering effects that inevitably surface.

As a YMCA coach, I appreciated the policy that every child gets an opportunity to play, putting the spotlight on the children. Irrespective of varying skill levels, each player was guaranteed equal time on the court. When the playing field is level, every child has a fair shot at success. This scenario necessitates that the coaches adjust and respond to the unique qualities each child brings to the game. At the YMCA, we catered to novices, as well as those, like my daughter, who've had a ball in their hands since they could walk.

I was coaching a team that included kids so young they seemed infantile. Some were so tiny that the smallest jersey enveloped them. Despite the YMCA not being an AAU league, some parents acted as though it was, harboring unrealistic expectations that their children would springboard from elementary school straight to the NBA. It may sound preposterous, but it's true! When it comes to their kids and sports, parents can sometimes be their worst enemy. They carry unreasonable and unachievable aspirations for their children. As a coach, I've witnessed novices lose their confidence after just one day of training, and more seasoned kids develop negative self-views due to their parents' unattainable expectations and fears.

Unfortunately, coaches can also have the same detrimental effect on kids. Young minds are invariably shaped by the personalities they're surrounded by. The trust placed in these figures is typically determined by their parents or the family environment they're in. My coaching approach revolved around fostering self-belief and a positive mindset in these children. I wanted to encourage them to be comfortable with making mistakes and to understand that errors can be constructive learning opportunities.

This story will showcase the triumph of optimism over pessimism, demonstrating how altering parental attitudes can swing the impact they have on their children, for better or worse. The team I was coaching was distinctive in that every child left with bolstered self-esteem and a positive mindset because they believed in themselves. I worked to lay this foundation with the hope it would endure throughout their lives. I'd always believed that it was adults, not the children themselves, who eroded their self-esteem and self-belief. I set out to turn that around. This team comprised ten children, including my own daughter, and I embarked on a fresh coaching approach, recognizing the critical role confidence plays in a child's development.

Identifying a child with low self-esteem always came easily to me. Because of confirmation bias, children's fears often mirror those of their parents, making it a parent's responsibility to uplift their child's confidence. Paradoxically, parental worry is what stunts a child's self-assurance before it has the chance to grow. This lack of confidence is the outcome of our inability to reconnect with our own inner child. My daughter was one of three female players on the team. I instilled in her the importance of self-belief and independent thought. It was clear to us that we were there to enjoy ourselves and strive for victory. While I could wax lyrical about my daughter's accomplishments, I have to bear in mind that the title of this book is "Dear Black Boyz," not "Dear Black Girlz," and so, for the purposes of this book, I will focus on the Boyz on this team.

The future will possibly see a book titled "Dear Black Girlz," celebrating the greatness of Black Girlz and their significance in our lives and the world at large. In the interim, some of this will be covered in a later chapter titled "Understanding a Woman's Perspective." These Boyz were selected because they each represent three distinct tiers of confidence. You might see yourself in one or more of these three Boyz. My eldest son is one of them.

Let's play a guessing game to add an interesting twist. Can you identify which of these Boyz is my son? I'll describe each one before revealing their identities. Base your guess on the level of confidence they exhibit.

I have two sons and a daughter. My daughter is the youngest, and is the best basketball player in the family, outshining her brothers by a long shot. This makes it easy: Ja Kobi wasn't on this team, and considering that one of the three Boyz is white, your guesswork is simplified. Fortunately, this reduces your options to the two Black Boyz.

As the season kicked off, the White kid's father served as my assistant coach. The boy was skilled at the game, though his father's harshness could be overbearing at times. In our narrative, let's name this Caucasian boy "Fear." There was another Boy who, intriguingly, seemed to flourish under his father's strict discipline. This Boy was the star player amongst the Boyz in the team, though he was still surpassed by my daughter. This Black Boy will be referred to as "Emotion." Lastly, there was a Boy with a more relaxed father who encouraged him to learn at his own speed. This Boy was not particularly skilled at basketball. He, also a Black Boy, will be referred to as "Moment." As this tale unfolds, our focus narrows down to Emotion and Moment. Brace yourself for an intriguing journey.

Intriguingly, we developed a rivalry with a team against whom we'd played only once in the previous season. This AAU 2nd and 3rd grade traveling team had grown into a formidable opponent after three years of playing together. Many players on my team were beginners, having never held a basketball prior to joining the team, and it was unclear how they would measure up against such a formidable adversary. I was told by some parents that this team, known as "The Monstars," had dominated the Y league for several seasons. With a staggering 40-point average margin of victory, they certainly seemed more mature than their counterparts, almost akin to sixth graders. The Y's policy ensured each child had equal playtime, regardless of the fees paid, upholding fairness at the core of its philosophy.

Our first encounter with The Monstars happened mid-season, during Game 5 of a ten-game series. The structure of the league allowed us to play against each team twice, and as luck would have it, we were slated to face The Monstars again in Game 10. Before our first face-off, my team was visibly intimidated by the size of their opponents. They looked terrified, their jaws agape in astonishment. In that game, I knew my daughter would have to step up for us to have any chance. Fearless as she was, she didn't disappoint. To put things into perspective, she scored over half of our total points, a staggering 20 out of 38. With a flawless 4-0 record, both teams entered this game undefeated. However, where The Monstars consistently outscored their opponents by a margin of 30 or more points, we only had a 10 to 12 point edge over the other squads. I knew we were up for a tough battle.

For the first quarter, I started my daughter, Moment, another girl, and two first-year players. To maintain a balance, I paired the stronger players with those less experienced, thus providing the beginners an opportunity to build their confidence. This approach ensured that all kids could enjoy their time on the court and savor the thrill of victory, which is essential for confidence building.

The Monstars boasted ten handpicked players who were as talented or even better than my daughter. Despite the challenge, my daughter was exceptional in the first quarter, scoring the first twelve points for our team, taking us to a 12-4 lead. She played with a prowess reminiscent of Stephen Curry. The Monstars were probably caught off-guard by her proficiency. Seeing his team falling behind, their coach, whom I had perceived as overconfident, quickly called a timeout. Despite having a strong team, he seemed to lack crucial coaching skills. A good coach nurtures their players while addressing areas of improvement, fostering confidence on and off the court. However, the Monstars' coach seemed to rely heavily on the children's talent, leaving them to develop their confidence without a proper support system.

Capitalizing on the Y's rules that did not allow stealing the ball unless it was passed, I taught my team to set up basic screens to create an open path to the basket. Children at this age generally struggle with complex defensive rotations, and since most coaches at this level weren't teaching these rotations, I knew we had an advantage. As we practiced our screens, I realized that my daughter and the other girl had developed a formidable partnership. The Monstars had no answer for this tactic, which we nicknamed "the screen."

Moment, fully engrossed in his own world, was enjoying the game despite occasionally fumbling. While he struggled with dribbling and catching, what he lacked in skill, he made up for his lack of experience with a positive spirit. He embodied the true essence of his name, living each moment to its fullest, regardless of the outcome. He stepped onto the court with the sole aim of having fun and doing his best, as his father always advised him. Always willing to step out of his comfort zone, Moment accepted growth irrespective of the outcome.

The second quarter commenced with my second team, with Fear and Emotion in the lineup. They were athletic for their age, but of a shorter stature. Fear, known for his full-speed attacks at the basket, had poor control over the ball and missed several layups. Each miss was met with growing frustration from Fear's father. Fear's natural confidence waned under the constant criticism from his father.

Fear was named so due to his fear of his father's critique, and his father was afraid of others' judgment on his son's mistakes. Meanwhile, Emotion, an excellent player and the second-best in the team, was held back only by his own temper. Having met his father, who seemed to have a confrontational attitude, Emotion's demeanor was more understandable.

Allow me to further illuminate on this matter since I have three Boy players each with different levels of self-assuredness. I will focus on the distinct aspects of their confidence, setting aside their individual skill sets for now. But before we dive into that, let's conclude the story I started with by detailing how the basketball game played out. At the close of the first quarter, we had a slight lead, with the score standing at 14-10 in our favor. All our points had been netted by my daughter and another girl on our team.

As the second quarter commenced, Fear, one of my Boy players, swiftly intercepted the cross-court inbounds pass. He charged towards the basket at full throttle but ended up missing the layup due to his overzealous sprint. He may have botched the first shot, but he made up for it by securing the rebound and scoring on the second attempt. This unexpected turn of events placated the Monstars—the opposing team—who assumed he would make the basket, and momentarily quelled the anger of his father. When I glanced at Fear's dad, his displeasure was palpable. He was irate about the missed layup, stating that Fear should've nailed it in the first attempt, negating the need for a rebound.

I empathized with his frustration, understanding that he wanted nothing but the best for his son. However, his aggressive approach was counterproductive. The joy and excitement had been sucked out of the game as Fear's father's unbridled anger demanded perfection from his son. Every mistake Fear made only chipped away at his confidence, especially when his dad lashed out at him. His father was adept at playing the killjoy, quashing his son's enjoyment and instructing him to get serious and focus. Fear would have been just fine had his father refrained from such harsh criticism, allowing him to learn from his errors. He was more afraid of not living up to his father's expectations than anything else.

Meanwhile, Emotion, another Boy, was eager and primed for the challenge. His father, always ready to stir the pot, had a chip on his shoulder. As Emotion dominated the second quarter and kept us in the game, his father became increasingly animated. His dad's exuberance was a bit excessive, but it was tolerated since Emotion was essentially carrying the team. With every point the Monstars scored, Emotion retorted with a counter score. His father was a dominant presence on the sidelines, ensuring everyone knew Emotion was his progeny. As we moved into the third quarter, our lead held at 24-18. The parents of our team members were reveling in the match, with the majority of the cheers and jeers emanating from Emotion's dad. The tide turned dramatically in the third quarter, which ultimately marked the inception of our rivalry with the Monstars.

We commenced the third quarter with possession of the ball. Emotion maneuvered the ball up the court, expecting Fear's screen. Fear executed a flawless screen, paving a clear path to the hoop for Emotion. But as Emotion leaped for the layup, a player from the Monstars shoved him mid-air, resulting in a hard fall. The referee instantly blew his whistle, indicating an intentional foul. This unsportsmanlike act sparked an altercation, with Emotion's father attempting to retaliate against the perpetrator. My intervention was the only thing preventing an escalation of the situation.

Despite the incident, Emotion concluded the quarter on a strong note. But the hostile environment that this foul had created irrevocably changed the dynamics of the game. With every subsequent foul call, the tension between the parents and players intensified, and the game spiraled out of control. By the end of the third quarter, we found ourselves trailing the Monstars 34-30. The momentum was now firmly with them as we entered the decisive fourth quarter. With the hopes of a comeback resting on her shoulders, my daughter stepped up once again. Although her efforts were commendable, they were insufficient to clinch victory, and we had to concede defeat, losing the game 42-38.

After the match, I assured the team that we would triumph over the Monstars the next time we faced them. Post-game, I had to prevent Emotion's father from initiating a brawl with the parents of the player who'd fouled his son.

Our final face-off of the season was against the Monstars, and we used the four subsequent games as practice for the ultimate showdown. When the day of the final match arrived, our record stood at 8-1, while the Monstars were undefeated at 9-0.

The final match against the Monstars was the highlight of the season. Everyone was hyper-focused, and regardless of the ups and downs in the game, we maintained a team spirit and positive attitude. Jumping forward to the fourth quarter to expedite the conclusion of the story, the entire match was a neck-to-neck battle. Finally, in the last two minutes, we found ourselves tied at 44-44.

My son, Tajion, whom I will now reveal as 'Moment,' was motivated to join the basketball team by his sister (Tya). In the final 30 seconds, the Monstars had just taken a two-point lead when Fear managed to create a clear path to the basket and sprinted towards it, but missed his shot. Emotion, however, was able to quickly respond and tied the game at 50-50.

In the final moments, the ball was intercepted by my daughter Tya, who spotted her open brother, Moment, and passed him the ball. Catching the ball off guard, Moment managed to score with just 5 seconds left on the clock. This victory, clinched by Moment's first and only game-winning shot, was the culmination of a season of self-belief and positive mental attitude.

Let me end with this thought: Achieving your desires requires patience, and hard work is a necessary complement to confidence. It's the journey that constitutes the dream, with the destination merely being the outcome of that journey. Confidence is a mental state that fosters belief in oneself. We must believe in ourselves in order for confidence to surface. If we can embrace success as a team, much like the team in this story, the world will be a more peaceful place. Remember, confidence and hard work are two sides of the same coin; you can't have one without the other. With confidence, you can conquer your fears, control your emotions, and live in the moment.

THE POWER OF CONFIDENCE

As we journey through these stories, one truth emerges with clarity: confidence is the foundation of personal growth, resilience, and success. Whether it's on the football field, in a one-on-one challenge, or on the basketball court, confidence shapes who we become and how far we go in life. But what exactly is confidence, and how do we nurture it in ourselves and others?

THE INNER AND OUTER JOURNEY OF CONFIDENCE

Confidence begins with knowing. It's rooted in a deep, unshakable understanding of who you are, your capabilities, and your purpose. This knowing isn't merely a belief but a certainty that comes from self-discovery, self-acceptance, and self-accountability. It's about being fully aware of both your strengths and vulnerabilities and knowing that you have the inner resources to meet any challenge.

This inner knowing is the foundation of confidence, but it must be expressed and validated in the external world without reliance on others' perspectives. Confidence is the force that drives you to act on what you know, to test your understanding, and to push your limits.

It's about showing up every day, doing the work, and proving not just to the world, but to yourself, that your knowing is justified. It's about embodying your knowledge through action.

THE SYMBIOSIS OF KNOWING AND DOING

The journey to confidence is a balance between inner knowing and outer doing. It starts with the internal work—developing a mindset that's grounded in self-awareness and self-certainty. But it doesn't end there. We must also take this knowing and bring it into the world, testing it, refining it, and confirming it through our actions.

Confidence is both the journey and the destination. It's not just about the outcomes of winning or losing, but about the unwavering certainty you carry within yourself as you face challenges and persist through adversity. It's about knowing your potential and consistently taking the steps necessary to realize it.

As you reflect on these stories, ask yourself: What is it that you know about yourself? How can you deepen this knowing? And how will you bring this knowing into the world, ready to act on it with full confidence?

Remember, true confidence is about knowing who you are and acting on that knowing every day. When you align your inner certainty with decisive action, you unlock a strength within yourself that can overcome any obstacle and achieve any dream. This is the power of confidence—a force that, once fully realized, makes you truly unstoppable.

Here are three questions a young Black Boy might ask himself about confidence after reading this chapter:

1. What do I truly know about myself, beyond what others expect or fear for me?
-This question encourages self-reflection on inner certainty and understanding, focusing on the importance of self-awareness over external influences.

2. How can I align my actions with the deep, unshakable knowing of who I am and what I'm capable of?
-This question challenges the reader to bridge the gap between inner confidence and outer actions, ensuring that their efforts reflect their true potential.

3. In what ways am I holding myself accountable to my own standards and pushing beyond the limits that fear and doubt try to impose on me?
-This question urges the reader to take responsibility for their growth, focusing on self-accountability and the ongoing process of confronting and overcoming fears.

Rise Above The Hustle
by Relly Rell

Dear Black Boyz,

CHAPTER TWO
ENERGY

A genius is someone who can take everything that seems impossible and solve it in a simple way. Your discomfort or sadness often represents your mind's plea to evolve beyond your existing way of thinking. Protect your energy by any means necessary, as Malcolm X eloquently stated, and do not allow negativity to infiltrate and occupy your mental space.

Every morning, we're granted two valuable gifts: a chance and a choice. The choices you make after you get your chance are what shape your life. Surround yourself with doers and not just talkers. If you find yourself ensnared in a harmful mindset, reinforced by negative energy, that's a clear signal to instigate change. Escaping from this negative sphere is the stepping stone toward a healthier outlook. Embrace change, as it brings enlightenment and can be integrated into every aspect of life. Remain steadfast, tenacious, and place unwavering trust in yourself. If you seek assistance and it's denied or not forthcoming, don't surrender. Continue your search for help, and when you find it, don't judge.

If there's one critical takeaway from this text, it should be this: INVEST IN YOURSELF! Invest in your mind, your body, and your dreams. Allocate resources to your intellectual growth, physical well-being, and aspirations. If you have a track record of detrimental habits, consider reading books, maintaining a regular workout routine, hydrating with quality living water, consuming nutritious food, and contemplating therapy.

When you channel your effort and focus into evolving into the person you aspire to be, the universe reciprocates. Investing in self-empowerment will aid you in identifying your life's purpose. Mastering your responses, exercising patience, keeping an open mind, and seizing opportunities as they arise will empower you to accomplish your heart's desires. Transform into the person you perceive in your reflections. This journey might necessitate introspection to better comprehend your psyche, but the energy you release into the universe will surely echo your self-perception. Your belief system and routines serve as mirrors reflecting your essence.

Energy is the inherent power and endurance necessary for sustained physical or mental activity. Strength signifies physical prowess, while vitality embodies vigor and a lively state of being. However, I urge you to focus more on your cognitive energy than your physical stamina. While identifying physical energy can be straightforward, mental energy is often more elusive and overlooked. Yet, it's is essential for finding peace and achieving true success.

An easy way to recognize physical energy is through the warmth of an embrace from a loved one, or the rush of adrenaline during a confrontation. However, the pinnacle of energy types is mental energy. The mind harbors solutions to all of life's riddles, hence, shielding your mind is crucial for survival. Protecting your mental energy is the greatest gift you can offer yourself—an everlasting gift that doesn't require any monetary investment.

All energy is transferable, but it is the mind that chooses what you accept as your truth. If you're doubtful about this concept, let me give you a vivid scenario using music as a backdrop. Growing up in the 1990s, when music was in its prime (in my humble opinion), I was deeply moved by the era's melodies. They relayed authentic emotions from the urban landscape in an uplifting manner, spurring me on. They emitted a positive vibe that resonated with me. Music of that decade served as a beacon during challenging times, offering a sense of solidarity. However, the energy imbued in contemporary music seems to differ significantly. Today's music often reflects a generation in desperate need of guidance, seemingly lost and seeking solace in substance abuse and escapism. Such messages are transmitted directly to this generation via music, a medium known for its profound reach into our souls and its ability to stir an array of emotions.

Have you ever listened to a piece of music that infused you with positive vibes, motivating you to strive for betterment? Or a song that incited aggression, solely because the lyrics resonated with the artist's emotions at the time of its creation? Energy, in any form, is transferable. So you'd be well served by cultivating a mindset imbued with positive and productive energy, for therein lies life's bounty. At the same time, you should also shun negative energy, which tends to destroy, rob, and deplete your vitality. Remember, it's within your capacity to transform this energy into something positive or negative.

Holding onto past burdens that breed suffering, stress, disappointment, anxiety, depression, and that stifle creativity, generates unhealthy energy. Negative energy represents a void where positive energy should exist. The only defense against this negativity is to counter it with positivity. Darkness is merely the absence of light. Safeguard your inner light against encroaching darkness. There's no room for darkness where light shines brightly. So be that beacon of light. Embody the universe's positive energy.

Your mental energy is your most valuable asset. It holds the answers to everything you desire in life. Protecting this energy isn't just a task; it's a way of life. It's about cultivating an environment, both within and around you, that nurtures growth, positivity, and resilience. When you protect your energy, you safeguard your potential, your dreams, and your ability to transform challenges into opportunities.

The universe is filled with energy, but only you have the power to transform this energy into a positive or negative outcome. Choose to be the light, choose to be the embodiment of positive energy in this world. This is your power, your responsibility, and your gift to yourself and to those around you.

NEGATIVE ENERGY

Transforming negative energy into a positive creative force within your mind requires a strong sense of self-worth; otherwise, you'll constantly be besieged by dark thoughts that could potentially wear you down. Such self-draining thoughts can lead you down a path of subconscious self-destruction. If you're not actively programming your life, life will program you. In all of your endeavors, the biggest challenge you'll face is yourself. A daily habit of nurturing a negative mindset will lead to an internal battle that spills over, causing damage to everything around you. Speaking the truth about others is straightforward, but accepting truths about yourself requires bravery. Energy, to me, manifests as emotions or thoughts. Allow me to clarify.

Pay attention to your intuition, as energy, and the sensations it invokes, is transferable. The expression "trust your gut," is a prime example of this energy transmission. When you heed this advice, your mind harnesses energy. Let's take, for instance, a moment when you experienced unsettling energy, perhaps when you entered a room or were around someone with a toxic aura. Most likely, you suddenly found yourself with a gut feeling that something was off. It was a natural, intuitive response from your mind. Unfortunately, we often ignore these gut feelings in favor of what we perceive with our eyes, particularly in distracting environments like parties. You could be too engrossed with familiar faces, or someone you've been romantically involved with, and this could lead you to disregard your inner thoughts and feelings. Subsequently, an alarming event like a shooting may occur, causing panic and regret for not trusting your gut feeling. Acknowledging a feeling or a thought is your first step towards understanding and harnessing energy. The crucial point is to believe in what you can't see. Faith, too, is a belief in the unseen. Trust that your intuition is there for a reason. You can't afford to ignore negative energy.

Positive energy can stand out starkly, similar to being the only Black Boy on an all-white basketball team in a predominantly white town. My experiences of being the lone Black Boy in class during my senior year in Logan, Utah, a primarily white town, inspired me to write this. Letting negative energy permeate your life will overshadow the positive energy. Negative energy acts like a sinister dark virus that aims to swallow all the light of your positive energy. It can snuff out the light in your mind, leaving you in total darkness, consumed by self-destruction. Learning to safeguard yourself from negative energy is crucial, as it can always infiltrate your life if you're not careful. It's your duty to protect your energy, and embracing peace in your life will always provide you with a fighting chance against your real enemy: negative energy. It's always ready to pounce, akin to a schoolyard bully, smashing any positive energy it encounters.

Your body is filled with energy, which manifests as a tingle. It's somewhat similar to Spiderman's Spidey-Sense, an ability to sense and respond to impending danger. Energy enables communication between your mind and body. Without it, you'll never find inner peace or unlock your mind's potential. Energy opens your mind to a gazillion new perspectives, aiding in finding peace and facilitating growth. Happiness is impossible without peace. Can you imagine life devoid of joy or serenity? Safeguarding your energy is essential for your mental well-being. If you wish to have a chance at peace, it's vital to protect your energy.

The key to protecting your energy lies in shifting your perspective. A fresh perspective can revolutionize your confidence, energy, communication, and emotions—the four pillars of peace and happiness. If the vision of perspectives I'm attempting to convey with these narratives hasn't quite resonated with you yet, please bear with me. I understand that things may not have clicked just yet. So I urge you to broaden your horizons and gain a new perspective by the end of this book. Stick with me on this journey, and I guarantee you'll reach the promised land of your own making. Your mind deserves transformation, and that transformation begins with a shift in perspective. Your mind is the portal to your achievement of anything you believe in. My wish for you is happiness, and my gift to you is a fresh perspective.

Let me share another story about protecting your energy and trusting your gut. Perhaps you forgot, so let me jog your memory. Remember when gunshots shattered the party ambiance, sending everyone into panic mode? Alright, now that we're back at the start, join me on this journey into the realm of negative energy. This is a glimpse of what kinds of calamities can sneak up on you when you disregard negative energy and fail to protect yourself. Clear your mind and approach this with your unique perspective.

Join me on this journey. Imagine you and I have been inseparable since fifth grade. We're heading to a nearby HBCU on athletic scholarships. As the country's top basketball player, I've chosen to attend an HBCU, and you've decided to join me. Now, back to the story.

As we stepped out of the car, the pulsating beats from a house party two doors down filled the air. Checking you out, I saw you were dressed to kill, exuding immense confidence. Your swagger appeared to have its own theme music. Your outfit paired perfectly with your new pair of fresh Jordans. And not to forget, your haircut was on point, and your cologne had an irresistible allure. Although we both knew I was the better-dressed one, we can argue about that later (lol). Entering the party, we were greeted by a jubilant crowd of beautiful Black Kings and Queens, immersing themselves in the vibrant culture. The music and the unity of our people had us mesmerized from the doorway. The party was everything we'd hoped for!

We both spotted Q, a childhood friend, surrounded by a couple of beauties in the middle of the dance floor. As the most talented rapper in town, Q was a local star, even without a record deal. We'd been fans since we discovered his talent in fifth grade. My attention then shifted to a couple of attractive girls nearby, so I nudged you to look. The time had come. With our heads held high, we walked past Q, exchanging quick greetings, heading towards the girls who'd been eyeing us.

But then, something felt amiss. My inner voice, always good at alerting me, noticed a man standing in the back, emitting a strange energy. His vibes didn't match the rest of the party. Our instincts had taught us to always survey our surroundings for anything unusual. Distracted by the allure of the beautiful Black Queens, however, you didn't notice the man.

"Why is he the only one wearing a hoodie?" my inner voice questioned. I attempted to draw your attention to him, but your focus was elsewhere. Overwhelmed by the captivating sight of the twerking queens, you dismissed my concerns.

Perhaps I was reading too much into it, I thought, choosing to ignore my gut feeling and enjoy the party. As the night progressed, I noticed Q still soaking up the limelight, when suddenly, my gaze returned to the man in the hoodie. He'd been standing at the same spot, eyeing Q intently.

"Isn't that the guy Q had a run-in with a few weeks ago?" I asked you, pointing at the hoodie-wearing man. My Spidey-Sense was on high alert now.

"We should leave. Something doesn't feel right," I warned you, but your response was dismissive. You didn't see what I saw, distracted by the energy of the moment and the enticing Queens.

Then it happened. Before I had a chance to reach Q, I was shot in the back. Everything around me moved in slow motion. I couldn't move, but I could hear the bullets whizzing by, making my heart race even faster. It felt like a movie I'd seen before, a storyline that was all too familiar. I knew what was going to happen next, but I couldn't do anything about it. I was helpless as my life force drained from my body. I couldn't even control my breathing. As I struggled to breathe, I reached out to my best friend, who was frozen in shock. He was looking at me, but he wasn't doing anything to help me. He didn't understand what was happening. I could see the fear in his eyes. The party had ended with gunshots, panic, and an image of me on the floor, bleeding out. The last thing I remember was you, my best friend, crying over my lifeless body, screaming my name. But I wasn't there. I was already gone.

Stay with me a little longer, there's another perspective to examine in this story. From your point of view, you saw me charging towards Q. Bang! The first bullet ricochets off the wall. The next four bullets will forever alter the course of your life. They'll tip your world on its axis because you were too engrossed to heed your instincts, senses, and surroundings. Bang! Bang! Q is shot twice, once in the chest, once in the neck. You see me, your closest friend since the fifth grade, fall on top of Q in an effort to shield him from the bullets. Bang, Bang! Two bullets hit my back as I try to save our friend Q. Despite the music still blaring, you manage to find your way through the ensuing chaos to reach Q and me. But the pandemonium, caused by terrified party-goers rushing to escape, makes it difficult for you to get to us.

Let's pause time for a moment. Take a look around. Your Boyz lie motionless on the ground, bathing in their own blood. Dead! You're in shock, distracted, mentally disoriented. That hooded man is still there, and now he's standing right behind you. Don't turn around because that Glock is now pressed against the back of your head… Bang! Everything fades to Black… In an instant, you too, are gone.

The news the following morning… At 2:22 a.m., three Black Boyz were shot dead at a house party. The police have said the shooting was gang-related. There are no leads at this time, but we'll update you as we learn more."

Gang-related? Is this how we're perceived? We were just there to enjoy the party. So, we arrived with potential and left as gang members? We, Q, you, and I, were all destined for greatness. Q was an aspiring music star, and you and I both had athletic scholarships. Something isn't adding up. Oh, but I forgot… nobody cares about our potential. The negative energy was palpable from the start, but we didn't listen. What if we'd left the party early? What if you had listened to me? What if Q had stayed with us? What if we had just skipped the party and stayed home, focusing on our dreams? An avoidable catastrophe claimed our lives, leaving behind countless unanswered questions that will forever remain a mystery.

We'll never meet the individuals we were meant to become in this world. Maybe we can share our potential selves in the afterlife, but not here on Earth, for our bodies now lie lifeless. The negative energy was present, but neither of us listened to my instincts. You were too absorbed in hormonal distractions, and Q never saw it coming. It's incredible to think we're gone. We were three Princes, not yet Kings, robbed of life too soon by someone fueled by envy, hate, and evident mental instability.

We had promising futures ahead. But from now on, we'll only be remembered as a statistic. Another ghetto tragedy… Three more Black Boyz caught in gang violence have been added to the local crime statistics. Protect your energy. When you sense negative energy, learn to acknowledge and respect it. Don't disregard your instincts. Don't ignore your intuition; alertness could save your life and the lives of those you care about. Just imagine if we'd left the party when I first sensed the unease, taking Q with us. Imagine if we'd stayed home that night, focused on our dreams—none of this would have happened. Imagine if I'd simply listened to my instincts when I detected negative energy. I had the power to save us all.

If you ever find yourself in my situation in this story, and your best friend is in your situation, I pray that you listen to your intuition when you notice negative energy and something "feels off." Recognize it and remove yourself from its presence!

Negative energy breeds a negative mindset, which leads to self-destruction. Learn to recognize the signs so you can protect your energy from negative influences. We all experience negative thoughts occasionally, but constant negativity deteriorates mental health, leading to depression, anxiety, and a darkened mindset. Positive thinking, on the other hand, improves mental health, reduces stress, and boosts cardiovascular health. Unfortunately, many of us are trapped in these negative thought cycles. To keep negative energy at bay, positive energy is required. Let your light shine bright enough to displace the darkness that negative energy brings.

POSITIVE ENERGY

Harnessing positive energy is a transformative journey that starts with a shift in perspective. It's about zooming out and seeing the bigger picture—the divine plan for your life's purpose. When things don't go as expected, when you face setbacks or unmet expectations, it's life nudging you towards something greater, something more aligned with your true path. Negative experiences can be powerful catalysts for growth if you transform them into tools of self-improvement.

Positive energy isn't just a concept; it's a force that can nurture your soul, drive out negativity, and bring peace into your life. The universe is filled with an infinite supply of positive energy, available to you whenever you choose to tap into it. Tapping into this energy is straightforward, and you have full control over how much you receive. But first, you need to clear your mind of negative energy—hatred, fear, anger, or doubt—and replace it with positive influences.

We all know the five senses: vision, hearing, touch, smell, and taste. But what about the sixth sense? I believe that our sixth sense is the mind—the part of us that enables awareness, thought, and emotion. The mind is the key to perceiving the world, and it's the control center for the other five senses. When you see, hear, touch, smell, or taste something, the mind interprets these sensations and translates them into feelings.

Imagine experiencing something impossible, something that "blows your mind." Or hearing a voice so powerful it gives you chills. These are examples of the mind at work, connecting physical sensations to emotions. Positive energy flows from these experiences, bringing peace and fulfillment. Feeding your mind with positive energy—through what you see, hear, touch, smell, and taste—creates a sense of harmony and contentment that fills every aspect of your life.

What if you could live every day with all your senses activated by positive energy? Imagine the peace and fulfillment you'd feel, the sense of completeness. Positive energy is the key to unlocking this state of being. It's the master ingredient that leads to peace within yourself and with the world around you.

Every day, make choices that feed your mind and senses with positivity. Listen to uplifting music, engage in conversations that build people up, and touch things that calm and soothe you. Surround yourself with beauty—whether in the form of art, nature, or the people you love. Choose fragrances that bring you joy, and savor food that delights your senses. By filling your life with positive energy, you create a barrier against the turbulence of the world, allowing your mind to find peace.

The mind is the true battleground, and the prize is your soul. The energy that dominates your mind determines the fate of your soul—whether it resides in a state of Heaven or Hell. But here's the thing: Heaven and Hell are not distant, physical places. They exist within your mind, shaped by the energy you cultivate. You can access Heaven without waiting for death—by filling your mind with positive thoughts and experiences, you can create a state of Heaven here and now.

We've been conditioned to believe that Heaven and Hell are places we go after we die, but what if they're actually states of mind that we experience in this life? What if the mindset you die with is the one you carry into the afterlife? If that's the case, wouldn't you want to cultivate a positive mindset now, to ensure peace and happiness both in this life and beyond?

Creativity is a gateway to this kind of thinking. It liberates your mind, transporting you to a realm of incredible ideas—a universe where all visions and dreams manifest. This is also the place where energy and peace exist, a Heaven within your own mind. Embrace your dreams, take chances, and step outside your comfort zone. These actions enrich your life, build your confidence, and fill your mind with positive energy.

Dreaming requires courage, and acting on those dreams requires conviction. Life is simple, even though many might tell you otherwise. Understand your mind, and you'll understand happiness. Recognize that life is temporary, but the mind—the sixth sense—is timeless.

Live your happiness now, love yourself now, stay present now, and simplify your life now. By doing so, you'll ensure that your mind is filled with positive energy, allowing you to experience Heaven on earth.

I used to fear death, uncertain about what lies beyond. We've all heard about Heaven and Hell as ultimate destinations, but what if they're just mental constructs shaped by the energy that occupies our minds? What if the soul's fate—whether it experiences Heaven or Hell—depends on the energy that dominates your mind in life?

In this contest between Heaven and Hell, between positive and negative energy, you have the power to choose. Choose to fill your mind with positive energy, to create your own Heaven here on earth. Your mind is the key to experiencing this Heaven, not just after you die, but every day of your life.

Positive energy is the force that fuels your dreams, drives your actions, and shapes your reality. It's the essence of creativity, the foundation of peace, and the gateway to happiness. Embrace it, nurture it, and let it guide you on your journey. Live each day with positive energy, and you'll find that Heaven isn't a distant place, but a state of mind that you can access whenever you choose.

PEACE

Peace signifies a state devoid of turmoil or unrest, a tranquil presence. This tranquility is a reflection of mental calmness and stability. When your mind is at peace, you're free from any disturbances. But let's think on this: Is it feasible to foster peace if we've been brought up in an environment devoid of opportunities? At first glance, it might seem impossible. Let me take you on a journey through my childhood, where peace was not something readily available but something I learned to cultivate.

I was raised in a world where Section 8 housing, food stamps, government-provided cheese, and free lunches were the norm. I vividly remember a time when the sewage line broke in our old home, literally flooding our carpets with two inches of crap. Yes, my childhood was literally engulfed in filth. We lived like that for over a year, exposed to countless unhealthy conditions. Such situations were daily occurrences for my siblings and me. An empty fridge was not uncommon, and we often relied on the generosity of others for food. At times, we lived without basic amenities like electricity and running water because we couldn't afford the bills.

I know what it's like to be jolted awake by a SWAT drug raid at my father's residence. I know the fear of being hounded by Bloods and Crips on my way home from school every day. I understand the profound sense of destitution and poverty. There's a difference between being broke and being poor. Being broke is a socioeconomic status; being poor is a state of mind. I didn't fully grasp the gravity of my situation until I moved to Utah, where I saw life from a completely different perspective.

Your environment shapes your life. The struggle carries its own unique charm, teaching you to be creative in the face of adversity and to value the happiness that comes from within. Growing up with struggle as the norm forces you to adapt to a life of often going without. It gives you a fresh perspective on life and teaches you to appreciate your inherent value, freeing you from the trappings of external circumstances beyond your control.

The real luxuries of life are the freedom to love, to have fun, to be happy, to be at peace, and to be true to yourself. And yet, these luxuries come free of charge. However, those who haven't struggled often find themselves paying for these things, metaphorically or literally, seeking happiness in material possessions. But true happiness is an intrinsic trait that can't be bought. It's often found among those who struggle because they've learned to seek happiness in things that are free—like love, family, friends, fun, peace, and the freedom to be themselves.

My aim in life, and the purpose of this book, is to liberate us from the constant social programming that dictates our lives. By doing so, we can shine brighter and spread peace throughout the world. It all begins with happiness. I want you to realize that happiness is free, and when you're free, you're happy. Happiness is a privilege for those who choose to believe in it. That's why I've made my choice to believe, and I invite you to do the same.

Those who struggle inherently possess an advantage over those who don't because they've had to find happiness in things that are free. Struggle compels you to seek happiness in life's simplest pleasures. If you explore the positive aspects of being Black, you'll find that struggle is a common thread. This struggle is a badge of honor in our DNA. Everything beautiful about us stems from our ancestors' triumph over enslavement. Struggle is coded into our DNA, but the problem arises when we accept struggle as a part of our culture while other cultures profit from our struggles. Depending on your perspective, struggle can be both a blessing and a curse.

Loving yourself and your mind is the key to setting yourself free and bringing peace to your world. Peace facilitates the acceptance of your own mistakes. The struggle will lead you to growth and peace, and as you mature, you'll find more peace. Visualize yourself as the Hyperion tree, the tallest tree in the world. As you grow, you learn to appreciate the tranquility that comes with uninterrupted growth.

Becoming the tallest tree in the world requires viewing your mistakes as stepping stones. I understand that making mistakes can be a bitter pill to swallow. No one enjoys being wrong all the time. But being aware that you may be wrong means you're open to challenging your beliefs, which is necessary for growth. Conscious growth leads to peace, and this peace, in turn, catalyzes further growth. If you're wrong, you're right, and if you're right, you're wrong. Always aim to be wrong so you can always be right. Let that idea seep in. This is how you become the tallest tree in the world.

Always being right shuts you off from new perspectives. Being wrong, on the other hand, opens up opportunities for new insights and growth. You can't grow if you're always right. Admitting you're wrong and accepting it allows you to evolve into that tallest tree—the Hyperion tree. Making mistakes is a prerequisite for nurturing happiness and peace within you. Invite peace into your life by considering different viewpoints apart from your own. When you share your light and love with the world, you'll outshine even the sun.

You've earned the right to enjoy happiness and peace. Don't postpone your happiness. You have the right to be happy and peaceful right now. Pause for a moment and ask yourself these questions: Who am I? Am I content with my life? Disregard the past and future for the time being and introspect: Am I happy? Am I at peace? Am I living in the past? Am I living in the future? Or am I living in the present moment? Staying in the present is the key to attaining happiness and peace.

Before you ask these crucial questions, however, you must be aware of your surroundings. Am I happy? Am I at peace right now? Consciousness refers to the ability to be aware of and respond to your surroundings. It signifies awakening. Your answers to these questions will determine your future course of action. If you can truthfully answer "yes" to "Am I happy?", it means you've understood the essence of life, and happiness and peace will continue to be your companions. If your honest answer is "no," it indicates that your internal struggles are overshadowed by a negative mindset. But even if this is the case now, the silver lining is that you can liberate yourself by becoming aware of your environment.

You have the option to live in peace and create your own paradise on Earth, rather than living in the Hell we currently find ourselves in. Peace is found through self-love, self-happiness, and self-awareness. Catering to these aspects yourself is a form of self-satisfaction that'll bring you peace. When you're at peace with yourself, you understand who you are. And when you know who you are, there's no need to defend your truth.

When you no longer have to defend yourself, you'll become open to new ideas and perspectives, leading to personal growth, happiness, peace, and acceptance of your own fallibility. Embrace the truth about yourself, free from emotional baggage, and you'll find room for self-improvement. Be present, introspect, and carve out your unique path, even if it contradicts your ingrained beliefs. By doing this, I assure you, happiness and peace will be your companions, even in the face of adversity.

Allow yourself the liberty to think independently. Allow yourself the freedom to love passionately, to envision your life just as you imagined. You now have the license to live a life filled with joy and tranquility. Love yourself enough to demand these things in your life right now. Why postpone? Inside you, peace resides. Liberate yourself to savor your personal heaven at this very moment.

No one wishes to leave this world with a heart heavy with sadness or without having experienced peace. No one wants to be forgotten after their departure. If you claim otherwise, you're fooling yourself. No one yearns to leave this world feeling their life is incomplete. So, why do we persist in living lives that are unfinished? If you believe happiness and peace are beyond your reach, then indeed, they will be. It's a self-fulfilling prophecy. You'll leave this world feeling a void, a sense of incompletion. Unless you alter your energy and embrace change, this sense of dissatisfaction may persist. So seize control of your life and strive for excellence. Be the captain of your ship and challenge yourself to reach your maximum potential. Be the titleholder, general manager, and chief coach of your own life. Take total control.

As the titleholder, you hold the reins of your destiny. As the general manager, you can eliminate the negativity that brings no value to your life. And as the chief coach, you can push yourself to clinch the championship of life. Remember, your decisions as the titleholder will have repercussions on the entirety of your life. Do you love yourself enough to seize victory every year? Don't settle for just seventeen championships like the Lakers and Celtics. Celebrate each year like a champion because you're worthy.

According to RZA, the Twelve Jewels of Life include Knowledge, Wisdom, Understanding, Freedom, Justice, Equality, Food, Clothing, Shelter, Love, Peace, and Happiness. First and foremost, a man must acquire Knowledge, Wisdom, and Understanding. Once equipped with these three, he can gain Freedom, but such Freedom must operate under the principles of Justice. A person has the freedom to act, but Justice ensures that all actions are measured and fair. Justice signifies the recompense or penalty for an action, ensuring equality, for all men are equal until disrupted.

A man needs necessities like Food, Clothing, and Shelter. What is food but sustenance for the body and mind? Clothing serves as a mantle of righteousness, and Shelter provides a sanctuary from negative energy and threats. Once these basic needs are met, what's left? Love. But can Love exist without Peace? And what are Love and Peace without Happiness? Happiness denotes self-satisfaction. P.E.A.C.E is an acronym for Positive Education Always Corrects Energy. Peace, in its essence, is the absence of turmoil.

Never procrastinate on pursuing your dreams; dreams are divine visions. You might awaken one day to find that you've relinquished your peace and happiness. Don't wait for salvation from an external source; it isn't forthcoming. Peace and happiness reside in the here and now. When you yearn for peace and happiness from the past, you gain only fleeting peace and happiness. If you seek peace and happiness in the future, you manifest elusive dreams. There's no harm in temporary happiness and peace. However, if you strive for peace and happiness in the present, you'll attain eternal peace and happiness.

Alter the unhappiness in your life and live in the present. Cherish life, love yourself, and have faith in your worth. Embrace life's freedoms. Happiness is attainable for all who learn to relish the journey rather than the destination. Commit to this today and embark on your journey. Make peace with yourself, be happy. Life is, after all, quite simple. When you master peace, you create a beautiful tapestry of life.

The Key to Unlocking and Mastering Your Energy: A Message to Black Boyz

To my young Black Kings, you carry within you an immense power—an energy that has been passed down through generations of strength, resilience, and brilliance. This energy is your birthright, the force that'll propel you to greatness. But to unlock and master this energy, you must first understand its nature, cultivate it with intention, protect it fiercely, and use it to shape your destiny.

UNDERSTANDING YOUR ENERGY

Your energy is the essence of who you are. It's the fire that burns within you, driving your dreams and ambitions. But like any powerful force, it can be either constructive or destructive. Understanding your energy means recognizing the different forms it can take—whether it's the positive energy that lifts you up or the negative energy that tries to pull you down.

In a world that often underestimates and misunderstands you, it's crucial to know the difference. Negative energy might show up as doubt, anger, or fear—emotions that are natural but can become barriers if left unchecked. By acknowledging these feelings and understanding their roots, you take the first step toward mastering your energy.

CULTIVATING POSITIVE ENERGY

The world may not always give you the support and validation you deserve, but that doesn't mean you can't create it for yourself. Cultivating positive energy is about feeding your spirit with what uplifts you. It's about surrounding yourself with people who see your potential and encourage your growth, engaging in activities that build your confidence, and filling your mind with thoughts that empower you.

Remember, you have the power to choose what influences your life. Whether it's the music you listen to, the books you read, or the conversations you have, every choice you make can either build you up or tear you down. Choose to fill your life with positive energy, and watch how it transforms your world.

PROTECTING YOUR ENERGY

In a society that often seeks to dim your light, protecting your energy is essential. You'll face challenges, negativity, and even people who don't want to see you succeed. But here's the truth: your energy is precious, and it's your responsibility to guard it.

Set boundaries with those who drain your energy or bring you down. Don't allow anyone to make you feel less than you are. Protecting your energy also means taking care of your mental and emotional health—finding peace within yourself and not letting the world dictate your worth.

TRANSMUTING NEGATIVE ENERGY

You'll encounter obstacles, and there'll be times when the world feels heavy. But the mark of true mastery is your ability to take that negative energy and turn it into something powerful. Transmuting negative energy is about taking control of your narrative. When life throws challenges your way, always do your best to see them as opportunities to grow stronger, wiser, and more resilient.

This is your superpower: the ability to transform pain into purpose, setbacks into comebacks, and obstacles into opportunities. By shifting your perspective, you can turn any negative experience into fuel for your journey. This is how you master your energy—by refusing to let the world break you and instead using every experience to build you up.

THE PATH TO MASTERY

Mastering your energy is the key to unlocking your potential. It's about becoming the King you're destined to be. When you master your energy, you take control of your life. You become the creator of your reality, the architect of your dreams, and the captain of your destiny.

This path isn't easy, of course, but nothing worth having ever is. It requires you to stay aware, to keep growing, and to never stop believing in yourself. But know this: you already have everything you need within you. You come from a legacy of Kings and Queens, of warriors and scholars, of people who overcame every obstacle and thrived. That same power runs through your veins.

YOUR JOURNEY BEGINS NOW

To all my Black Boyz reading this, know that you're powerful beyond measure. You have the strength, the intelligence, and the spirit to conquer anything you set your mind to. Mastering your energy is the key to your success, your peace, and your happiness. It's the key to becoming the man you're meant to be.

Don't let the world tell you who you are—define you for yourself. Use the lessons in this chapter to unlock and master your energy. Protect it, nurture it, and let it guide you to greatness. The world is yours for the taking. Now go out there and show them what you're made of.

Here are three questions a young Black Boy might ask himself about mastering and

understanding his energy, after reading this chapter:

1. What are the sources of my energy—both positive and negative—and how do they influence my thoughts, emotions, and actions?
-This question encourages self-reflection on what drives you forward or holds you back. It helps you identify the people, environments, and habits that either uplift or drain you, guiding you to make conscious choices about where and how you invest your energy.

2. How do I protect my energy when faced with negativity, doubt, or challenges?
-This question prompts you to think about the strategies you can use to guard your energy. It encourages you to recognize your boundaries, develop resilience, and learn ways to transform negative experiences into lessons or fuel for personal growth.

3. Am I using my energy to create the life I envision for myself, or am I letting others dictate my path?
-This question pushes you to consider whether you're in control of your energy or if you're being influenced by external forces. It helps you to take ownership of your destiny, align your actions with your goals, and live authentically according to your values and dreams.

The Purpose of Love
by Relly Rell

CHAPTER THREE
COMMUNICATION

Communication is the transactional process of creating and sharing your personal meanings with those of others. It's the bridge that connects us to others, and yet it's often where so many of us falter. To communicate effectively, you must first shed your preconceptions and be willing to temporarily set aside your own perspective. Without doing so, communication becomes a battleground of egos rather than a genuine exchange of understanding.

Communication flows in two complimentary streams: nonverbal and verbal. Nonverbal communication, such as body language or facial expressions (among the other categories indicated below), usually serves as our initial data point when engaging with others. These forms of expression tend to be the first things we recognize when we encounter someone new. The way your body moves, the expressions on your face, the feelings you convey through your vocal intonation, the way you present your physical appearance, and the ways you manage your personal space—these can convey emotions even before a word is spoken. Verbal communication, on the other hand, is your message content (the vocabulary or word choices you make in order to convey the personal meanings you wish to share), and is remembered through the nuances in a person's voice, including inflection and tone. Both of these aspects of communication activity methods convey emotions, but they're often misunderstood or conflated, leading to a breakdown in communication.

I once believed I was a great communicator. I thought that because I could talk without yelling, cursing, or getting overly emotional, I had mastered communication. But that belief was shattered when I met my wife. It was through our relationship that I truly began to understand the depth of communication, and I realized just how much I still had to learn. I'll circle back to that later when I discuss relationships in more detail.

Growing up, our communication skills are shaped by those we interact with the most—parents, siblings, friends, and authority figures. For many of us, these early interactions teach us more about what not to say than how to express ourselves effectively. When you're a kid, no one really cares about your opinion, and this often teaches you to silence your voice. Then, when you become a teenager and start to find your voice, you're suddenly labeled as hard to deal with. This is because your newly found voice, which had been dormant for years, has finally surfaced, but you were never taught how to use your incredibly powerful and creative voice effectively.

For many of us, our only examples of communication come from being told what to say and what not to say. We're taught to always respect our elders, but if we disagree or stop believing what they taught us, we're considered disrespectful. I've never understood how a disagreement could be labeled as disrespect. And if you dare to question those elders, you're hit with the famous saying, "It's not what you say, but how you say it." But I've always wondered if some parents ever stop to think about where we learned how to say "it" in the first place.

Effective communication can only be learned or taught, and if we only witness non-effective communication growing up, that becomes our default practice until we unlearn it. It took me 37 years to begin overcoming the bad communication habits I was programmed to believe were effective. I only learned how to communicate effectively once I stopped caring about my own perspective or about being right. Growth requires that you be okay with being wrong, and strengthening your communication practice is the perfect example of how you can be okay with being wrong.

Think of every argument you've ever had. Without even knowing you or the topic of your disagreement, I can guarantee that I know why you were arguing. Arguments are almost always about who is wrong or right, about being misunderstood, or about defending your truth. Now, imagine if you didn't care about being wrong or right. Imagine if you were okay with being misunderstood and didn't feel the need to defend your truth. How many arguments would you still have had?

The most important communication skill to master is communication with yourself. Self-communication is the ability to sit in your thoughts without needing to explain yourself. It's the practice of keeping your thoughts and feelings inside your mind without letting your mouth speak up for you when emotions get involved. Emotions are natural, instinctive states of mind-derived from one's circumstances, mood, or relationships with others. But once emotions intensify beyond a certain point, they can be the killer of everything. This is why self-communication is so critical—if you can't communicate effectively with yourself, you'll struggle to communicate effectively with anyone else.

Self-communication is something you have to practice daily. It starts with being honest with yourself. Honesty is freedom from deceit and untruthfulness. Without honesty, self-communication is impossible to understand. Your negative emotions will always surface and kill any progress or growth that you've already obtained. Let's go back to any argument you've been involved in and do a deep dive into it. Why do we fight to be right in the first place? Why do we even care about making people understand our perspective? I can tell you why—it's because we're carrying a lot of trauma and insecurities from our past.

The defenses we deploy when those negative emotions surface are the shields we put up so that we don't have to face our insecurities. Instead of being honest with ourselves, it's easier to point the finger or the blame in another direction to take the spotlight off ourselves. This is why we feel the need to fight to be right all the time—it keeps the attention off our true problems. Once you believe you can do it, you'll discover that you've always had the power to hold yourself accountable for finding your greatness within by simply being honest with your emotions. Ask yourself why these negative emotions are coming up and why you care so much about being right. A lot of it probably comes from not being heard or being misunderstood as a child.

But why do we care? I believe that a lot of our insecurity comes from the feeling of being wrong and the negative effects that came from being wrong as a child. We've been programmed to believe—from our parents, schools, unjust laws, and the workplace—that being wrong is a bad thing. In all these places, being wrong comes with consequences that make you feel like that same little kid who was never heard. No one likes feeling like a little kid because it reminds us of the times when our voice was silenced. We're quick to remind everyone that we aren't little anymore, that now we have a voice, and that little kid inside of us wants revenge on anyone and everyone. But being wrong doesn't have to have a negative effect. It can actually be a positive thing to accept. When you learn how to deal with the little kid inside you, then you can be honest with yourself at all times. The little kid represents all of your unheard and unexpressed emotions, and each emotion represents a different kid. So every time they surface, self-communication is needed to let those little kids know that it'll be okay.

Being able to communicate with that little kid internally gives him confidence not to take things personally. Accepting being wrong is a good thing because the kids get to be themselves without any judgment. Sitting in silence keeps the little kids safer than if you defend them to the world. Defending yourself actually reveals all your insecurities to those who would use them against you. Be honest with yourself about your insecurities so that the little kids that live inside of you can grow up to be what you see in the mirror. Pay more attention to the things you're defending yourself against, and you'll find all your insecurities. Pay more attention to your complaints, and you'll hear what you desire most out of life. Pay more attention to the lies you knowingly tell people, and you'll find the lies you tell yourself.

The conversations you have on the outside, defending yourself, are the issues you're dealing with on the inside. We need to have those tough conversations with ourselves and treat the little kid that lives inside us like an innocent child. Your inner child needs to hear something positive from you every day because he's waiting to hear from you. Your inner child is directly connected to the universe, and once you understand that, then you have no choice but to relax your own perspective. Sit in silence and get to know yourself so you can reintroduce yourself to yourself.

We're all Black Boyz living in a world that wants to silence us. But they can no longer silence you because you've found your voice.

UNDERSTANDING A WOMAN'S PERSPECTIVE

Mastering communication isn't just about expressing your thoughts; it's also about understanding the perspectives of others, especially women. For a Black Boy, the first and most formative relationship with a woman is often with his mother, or in her absence, a grandmother. These early relationships shape how we perceive and interact with women throughout our lives. My own mother profoundly influenced my understanding of women, and not knowing my grandmothers left a void that also shaped my perspective.

The relationship between a Black Boy and his mother can be complex, particularly during the tumultuous period of adolescence. This is a time of self-assertion and confusion, where every new sign of manhood, like the first appearance of pubic hair, marks a shift in the dynamic. As a teenager, I perceived my mother as constantly nagging and complaining, always focused on what I was doing wrong. She held her children to high standards, a trait I later recognized as rooted in deep care and love. But at that time, her constant critiques became something I despised—a pet peeve that I carried with me into adulthood.

It wasn't until I was 37 and a father myself that I truly understood my mother's way of communicating. Observing how my wife interacted with our son, and seeing his frustrations mirror my own, I realized that I was witnessing a cycle. I saw in my son the younger version of myself, trying to protect him from what I perceived as the nagging and complaints of his mother. But my perspective shifted drastically when my wife, exasperated, asked, "When do I get the benefit of the doubt?" Her words—and the painful silence that followed—opened my eyes to a new understanding of communication.

The revelation wasn't just about what my wife said, but how she said it. I began to understand that true love involves surrendering your own perspective to truly grasp someone else's. What I'd dismissed as nagging and complaining were actually expressions of what mattered deeply to her. It was her way of communicating her needs, desires, and concerns. This realization changed everything for me. I began to see that there might be more effective ways of communicating, but understanding her perspective helped me understand myself better, too.

This newfound understanding revolutionized my interactions with the women in my life. I passed this knowledge onto my son, teaching him that complaints are often expressions of unfulfilled desires and needs, not personal attacks. I began to appreciate the value of listening to complaints, seeing them as opportunities to understand what the women in my life truly wanted and needed. What I had once despised became a key to understanding women better. With this shift in perspective, communication with the women in my life became less challenging and more fulfilling.

However, effective communication is about more than just understanding; it's equally about listening without taking things personally or as a judgment of your worth. Listen, think, respond—in that order. My wife taught me the importance of truly listening. The next time you interact with a woman, try listening without interjecting your viewpoint or taking it as a reflection of your character. It's evident to others when you're not listening, especially when your responses begin with "but." We've been trained to speak, yet listening is often undervalued and underpracticed, resulting in a world overflowing with opinions but lacking true understanding.

A genuine relationship is where two imperfect people persevere with each other, even when it's difficult. Communication is central to such a relationship. Women are often portrayed as complicated, and I believed this until I started truly listening. I learned to pay attention to the women around me, especially in my relationships. Every man needs a woman who'll challenge his thinking and inspire open-mindedness. In any relationship, it's vital to confront and resolve your past traumas so they don't get triggered by the words of a woman, making you revert to your vulnerable, inner child. Before committing to a relationship, it's essential to share a common foundation, including a complimentary belief system and mental state. Without this, the relationship is as precarious as a house built on a beach's sandy bed. This idea is particularly poignant for Black Men and Black Women. Listening to a Black Woman can be transformative for a Black Boy, teaching him about himself and life. The perceived inferiority of Black Women is a historical scar from our ancestors' enslavement, with bigoted divide-and-conquer strategies perpetuating this view.

A spiritual connection with a Black Woman, however, can change this narrative. It's a beautiful bond that comes with a deep mental connection and shared experiences, characterized by understanding, shared interests, and chemistry. Such a connection allows for effortless communication and a newfound understanding of a woman's perspective. This understanding can revolutionize your communication with everyone.

Communication should be about fostering understanding and self-improvement. Rather than using it to defend or tear down, communication should be about sharing dreams and offering encouragement. It's about promoting love rather than hatred, and fostering positive energy. Remember, how we communicate with ourselves and others reflects our self-perception. Mute your perspective, be honest with your inner child, and take responsibility, and you'll find that communication naturally improves.

In the end, understanding a woman's perspective is not just about better relationships with women; it's also about building a better relationship with yourself. When you can see beyond your own viewpoint and truly listen to another's, you'll unlock the potential for deeper connections, not just with women but with everyone in your life. Communication becomes not just a tool for expression but a bridge to understanding, healing, and growth.

The Power of Communication and Knowing

As we conclude this chapter on communication, it's essential to understand that the words we speak, especially the ones we direct at ourselves, hold immense power. Communication isn't just about the words we exchange with others; it's about the internal dialogue that shapes our self-perception, our actions, and ultimately, our lives. For Black Boyz, mastering this internal and external communication is crucial for self-discovery, growth, and empowerment.

The Words We Speak to Ourselves

The way we communicate with ourselves sets the tone for everything else. If your inner dialogue is filled with doubt, fear, and negativity, it'll manifest in how you interact with the world. But if your self-talk is rooted in self-awareness, self-respect, and self-love, it creates a foundation of confidence and strength. It's important to remember that your words are a reflection of what you know about yourself. This knowing, this deep-rooted understanding of who you are, is the cornerstone of your identity.

As Black Boyz, we must be intentional with our words, especially the ones we say to ourselves. Every time you look in the mirror, every time you face a challenge, make sure to remind yourself of who you are. Speak words that affirm your worth, your abilities, and your purpose. This isn't about empty affirmations, but about reinforcing the truth you know within yourself. The more you align your words with your inner knowing, the more powerful and effective your communication will become.

Tying Communication Into Your Innate Knowing

True communication is more than just exchanging words; it's about expressing and affirming what you know to be true. When you speak from a place of knowing—knowing your value, your capabilities, and your purpose—your words carry weight. They have the power to inspire, to heal, and to transform. This is the essence of effective communication: it's not just about being heard, but about being understood, and more importantly, about understanding yourself.

Knowing yourself allows you to communicate with clarity and authenticity. It gives you the confidence to speak your truth without fear, to listen without judgment, and to engage with others in meaningful ways. When you communicate from a place of knowing, you aren't just exchanging words; you're sharing a part of yourself, building connections that are grounded in mutual respect and understanding.

The Journey Forward

As you move forward, remember that communication is a journey—a continuous process of learning, growing, and refining how you interact with yourself and with others. It's about knowing when to speak and when to listen; when to assert and when to surrender. It's about balancing your inner knowing with the external realities of the world you navigate.

For Black Boyz, this journey is especially important. In a world that often tries to silence or misunderstand you, knowing yourself and mastering communication becomes a powerful tool for asserting your identity and carving out your path. Your words have the power to shape your reality, to uplift those around you, and to challenge the narratives that seek to define you.

So, as you continue this journey, I encourage you to speak words that reflect your deepest knowing. Let your communication be a testament to your growth, your strength, and your unwavering commitment to becoming the best version of yourself. Remember, the most important conversation you will ever have is the one you have with yourself. Make it count.

Final Reflection

In the end, communication is about more than just words—it's about connection, understanding, and truth. It's about aligning what you know with how you express yourself and how you listen to others. When you speak from a place of knowing, when you listen with the intent to understand, and when you communicate with honesty and integrity, you not only empower yourself but also those around you.

For Black Boyz, this is not just a skill—it's a survival tool, a means of thriving in a world that may not always care to see your full potential. Embrace the power of your words, trust in your knowing, and let your communication be the bridge that connects you to your highest self and to the world in a way that's true, powerful, and transformative.

Here are three questions that Black Boyz should ask themselves to help deepen their understanding of communication:

1. Am I truly listening to understand, or am I just waiting for my turn to speak?
-This question encourages self-reflection on how well you listen during conversations. Understanding others requires the empathic approach to active listening, where the focus is on comprehending the speaker's perspective rather than preparing your response.

2. How do the thoughts I think within myself shape the way I communicate with others?
-This question prompts you to consider the impact of your internal dialogue on your external communication. Positive self-talk can lead to more confident and effective communication with others, while negative self-talk can undermine it.

3. Do I communicate with authenticity, expressing what I truly know and feel, or do I hold back to protect myself?
-This question challenges you to assess the honesty and authenticity of your communication. Speaking from a place of knowing, rather than fear or insecurity, leads to more genuine and impactful interactions.

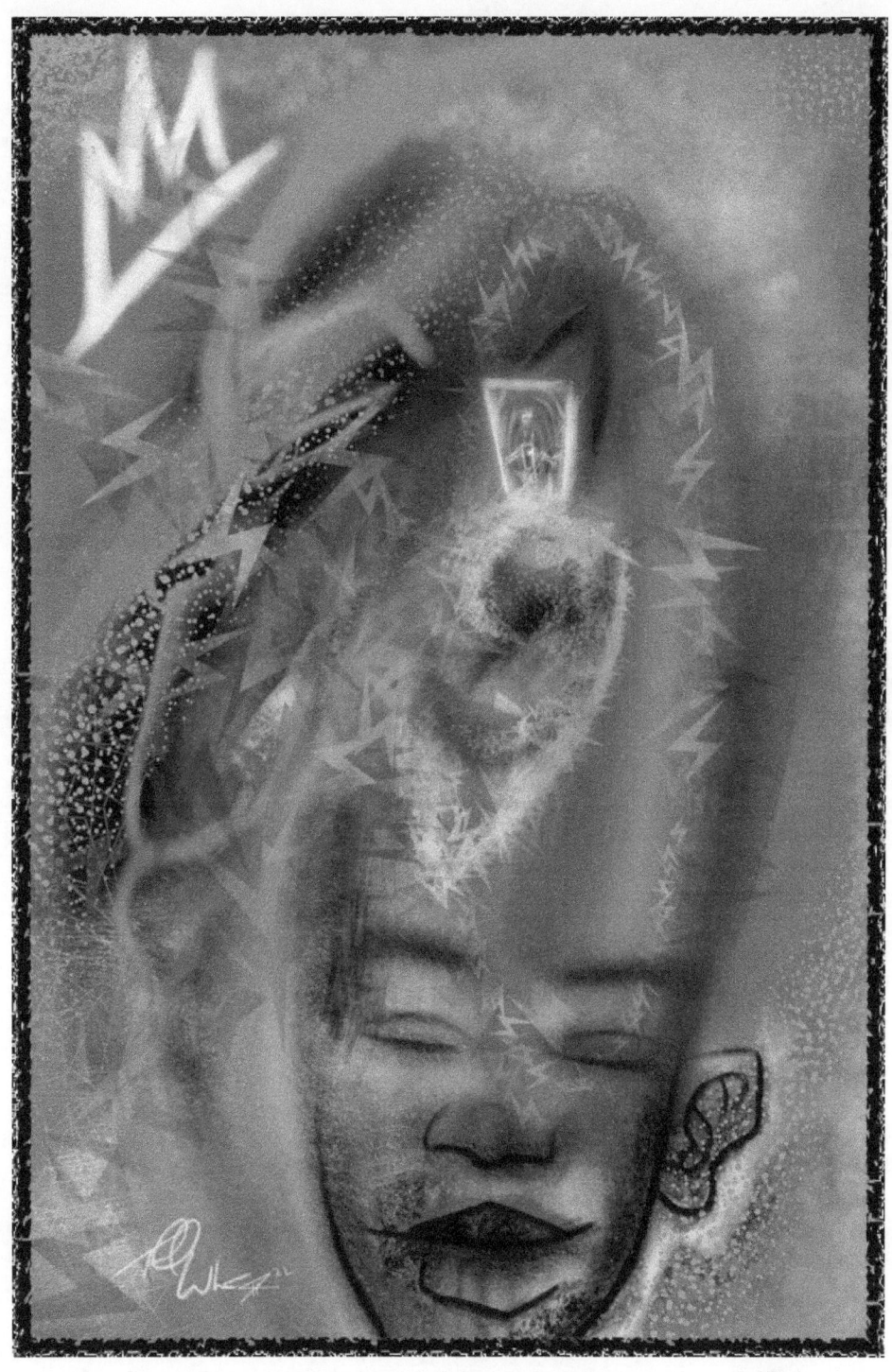

Selfless
by Relly Rell

Dear Black Boyz,

CHAPTER FOUR
EMOTION

A mind that has yet to mature often shies away from accountability, held captive by its own negative emotions. These self-limiting emotions represent the youthful aspects of our psyche, disrupting our tranquility and clarity. To truly understand and appreciate oneself, you must first bravely explore your emotional landscape. This chapter is about confronting those emotions head-on and guiding them towards maturity and peace.

Imagine your emotions as a group of inner children, each vying for your attention, each with their own personality and influence on your state of mind. Now, visualize embarking on a journey through the expansive universe of your mind, where these emotions reside. Your mind is like an endless expanse, a limitless canvas where these inner children exist and interact.

In this narrative, we're the elder brothers, guiding these emotions. There are five such brothers, each named after the emotions they personify: Disappointment, Sadness, Anger, Doubt, and Love. Love, the eldest, embodies our true essence, the core of who we are. Love is willing to make sacrifices for his younger counterparts, striving to lead them towards happiness and protecting them from Fear, which we'll encounter later in this journey.

Love is confident, exuding positive energy and acting as a role model for his younger brothers. However, the constant responsibility of caring for them can drain even Love's strength. This journey through the mind is not just about navigating these emotions but about recognizing the delicate balance between them and the impact they have on our overall well-being.

Our destination is the subconscious mind, a realm where emotions can either thrive in harmony or become trapped in prisons of negative perspectives. As we embark on this journey, I encourage you to keep an open mind, ready to embrace new insights and perspectives. Every experience, every emotion has a purpose, just as every journey has a destination.

In the subconscious mind, the brothers—Disappointment, Sadness, Anger, Doubt, and Love— each face their own struggles. Disappointment might feel abandoned or let down, while Sadness carries the weight of grief and loss. Anger, often misunderstood, seeks justice but can easily be consumed by rage. Doubt questions everything, even the validity of its own existence. Love, though strong, sometimes sacrifices too much of itself for the sake of its brothers.

As you witness these emotions interacting and evolving, you'll begin to understand how they shape your thoughts, decisions, and actions. You'll see how Love, despite its strength, needs to be nurtured and supported just as much as the other emotions. And you'll recognize that each emotion, no matter how challenging, plays a crucial role in your personal growth and development.

The Power of Perspective

This journey is about more than just understanding your negative emotions—it's about transforming them. By shifting your perspective, you can begin to see these emotions not as obstacles but as opportunities for growth. Imagine if you had the power to construct your paradise on Earth, your personal heaven. What would it look like? How would your emotions contribute to that vision?

As Black Boyz, we need to remember our inherent worth in this world. This book is designed to trigger an immediate positive shift in your life (once you've committed yourself to bravely and consistently practicing the principles I'm sharing with you), helping you to see that happiness and peace of mind aren't just distant dreams but realities you can achieve here and now. Heaven on Earth isn't some far-off place—it's a state of mind, a state of being that you can cultivate through self-love, acceptance, and emotional maturity.

Heaven, although unseen, is a state of euphoria, peace of mind, and fulfillment derived from engaging in what you love. Allow me to share some of my experiences while residing in this earthly paradise. I've been frequenting Heaven lately, surrounded by people who reciprocate my love. The emotional bond formed with these beings is truly inspiring, providing spiritual interactions and mutual encouragement. Every day, I discover new facets of myself. There seems to be a surge of positivity and creativity that fuels me every day, helping me pen this book.

It's now 2024, and I've been working on a cartoon called City of Hoops since the close of 1999, marking 24 years of dedication. My team and I have experienced some extraordinary developments in recent months. Relly Rell Studios has crafted something unique for the teenage demographic. Depending on when you're reading or listening to this book, Relly Rell Studios might be familiar. If not, you're joining me at the start of my journey, and there's much more to come. So, let's explore this journey together and unearth the potential that lies ahead. Once you find your Heaven on Earth, I only ask that you leave a trail for the next Black Boy or Black Girl to follow. Share your thoughts about "The Devil's Perspective" and the possibilities that emerge with a shift in perspective. Now, let's embark on our journey titled "Heaven Here On Earth."

As we conclude this chapter, remember that even your negative emotions aren't your enemies—they're your guides. Each one has a lesson to teach, a message to deliver. By acknowledging and embracing all of your feelings, you'll accelerate the maturation of your mind, allowing you to live in a state of peace and fulfillment sooner rather than later.

Take this journey with me, and let's see what's possible. The only thing I ask is that when you do find your Heaven on Earth, tell as many people as you can about what's truly possible when they adopt a new perspective. By embracing your emotions and guiding them with Love, you can create a life filled with joy, purpose, and peace—a life that feels like Heaven on Earth.

Heaven Here on Earth

Love was a courageous, fearless teenage warrior of the dark, destined to become the Hero who would conquer Fear. In the mystical World of Minds, a realm where emotions intertwine and hold power, Fear posed a persistent threat, embodying pure negativity. The Day of Consciousness marked the advent of emotions in this world, giving Fear his first opportunity to infiltrate and influence the World of Minds.

The gatekeepers of the World of Minds were three guardians known as the Angels of Truth: Dream, Hustle, and Inspire. Their sacred duty was to allow Fear, on the Day of Consciousness, to enter the realm and exert influence over any emotion. Fear, relentless and insidious, thrived on the emotions that pulsed through the World of Minds, a place sculpted after the Heavens themselves.

For this world to endure, its sustenance depended on the teachings of Truth from the Angels. Love, always vigilant of Fear's potential threat, first encountered Fear on his own Day of Consciousness. Unlike other emotions, Love remained the singular force that Fear couldn't overwhelm. Love, fearless and authentic, ruled over DreamVille, the mightiest of all villages in the World of Minds. His village, populated by Love-infused warriors, upheld the Silent Truth, a bulwark against Fear. In this world, a mole named Flesh, who had the power to subvert DreamVille and the Silent Truth, formed a dark alliance with Fear. Flesh, an ancient wizard from the Physical World, was the only outsider granted access to DreamVille. He earned this privilege through his skill in providing worldly pleasures from his homeland. Flesh, armed with the teachings of lower-tier Lust, was the only entity capable of reaching and manipulating Love. Fear needed Flesh to unravel the secret instructions of DreamVille, allowing him to control not just emotions, but the entire World of Minds.

Fear knew that the only ones capable of overthrowing their elder brother Love were the quadruplets—Disappointment, Sadness, Anger, and Doubt. Without Love, Fear could reign supreme in the World of Minds, granting him enough power to obliterate DreamVille's dauntless warriors. The Positive Energy Temple of Life, a sacred place where the Silent Truth was taught, guided these warriors in their daily meditation rituals, performed each morning upon awakening.

Fear anticipated more than just the quadruplets' Day of Consciousness. On that fateful day, all of DreamVille's mighty warriors assembled, with Love, crowned and adorned, leading the congregation. As Love stood at the forefront, awaiting his brothers, Fear and Flesh made their covert entry through the Gates of Truth. To gain entry into the World of Minds, Fear had to recite the three truths upheld by the Angels: Confidence, Energy, and Communication.

Upon gaining entry, Fear established himself in the Negative Energy Village of the Lost, also known as Lost Dreams. Love had previously demolished a small section of the World of Minds, named Lost Dreams, to protect the realm from Fear's influence. In exchange for delivering the quadruplets to him, Fear promised Flesh his daughter's hand in marriage. Flesh, yearning for pleasure, found the deal too enticing to resist. Thus, Flesh, armed with a cart of Lust, entered DreamVille without raising suspicion.

With the best entertainment from the Physical World and a feast of exotic cuisines, Flesh successfully distracted Love and the villagers. While everyone was indulging in the festivities, Flesh managed to lead the brothers out of DreamVille, one by one, to meet Fear. Lured by promises of kingship, the brothers—Disappointment, Sadness, Anger, and Doubt—left DreamVille. Flesh spun a false tale of Love's betrayal, how Love had expelled Fear and usurped the throne.

Disappointment, the youngest, was the first to be enticed. Upon learning of their father's supposed unjust fate, the brothers were filled with resentment towards Love. Their belief was further cemented when they finally saw their supposedly dead father, Fear, still alive. Fear then revealed the true meanings of their names, triggering their negative emotions. Love, realizing his brothers' absence, cornered Flesh, who confessed their whereabouts. Knowing what had to be done, Love commanded his warriors to kill Flesh before setting off to save his brothers.

Lost Dreams, the Negative Energy Village, was a graveyard for dreams and a cradle for nightmares, where emotions turned toxic. Fear, with his brief reign, had indoctrinated his sons into believing in their negative emotions. Love arrived at Lost Dreams and appealed to his brothers to recognize their true selves, but it was too late. Fear's teachings had already taken root, and negative emotions threatened to engulf the World of Minds. Love's brothers, fueled by their father's hatred, were ready to unleash their negativity onto Love. Love's plea to his siblings was met with hardened hearts. He recognized that to halt the spiral of Hate, he might have to eradicate them and their Father. Love understood that the only way the World of Minds could persevere was if he eradicated Fear and the damaging emotions his brothers harbored. With a final attempt, Love entreated his father, Fear, saying, "Fear, you are an emotion born from the suspicion of harm, peril, or threat. Your essence thrives on inflicting pain, and your presence endangers this world. I am Love, and without me, you cease to exist. I thrive in all you loathe, and all you love." To this, Fear retorted, "I find no joy in Love."

"But you do," countered Love. "You find joy in Lust, in Gluttony, in Greed, in Sloth, in Envy, in Wrath, and in Pride. Love has always been at the heart of your harmful teachings. Fear, your combat against me is fueled by your fear of me. I am Love! Fear, you are the one truly lost and fearful. You seek to pit my brothers and the World of Minds against each other and me."

A puzzled expression claimed Fear's face, and the silence that ensued among his brothers reflected their awakened realization. The siblings awaited Fear's reply with bated breath. "Your brother, Love, is deceptive. His teachings bring no benefit. Love is not Patient. It is not Kind. Love holds onto every injustice. I stand against Love. I stand against you, and Love must perish today."

With these words, the energy in the room shifted back to Fear and the inevitable conflict. With a somber voice, Love pronounced right before lunging at Fear and his brothers, "Love can only be realized within oneself for happiness to truly exist." Love had foreseen this day, yet he had patiently waited. He was ready to relinquish his love for his brothers to preserve Positive Energy in the World of Minds. With a swift, decisive stroke of his sword,

Love ended Fear and his brothers, their malevolent emotions trailing from his blade. "I am Love," he proclaimed to the Lost Dreams. "Anyone against Love and peace opposes me, and thus, opposes themselves. You will pay the price for the greater good, peace, and prosperity."

In "Heaven Here on Earth," the above story teaches that to protect your mind and create a life filled with peace and positivity, sometimes you have to make tough choices. Love, the main character, realizes that in order to keep the World of Minds—a symbol for your thoughts and emotions—safe and peaceful, he has to let go of or even "destroy" his brothers, who represent negative emotions like Disappointment, Sadness, Anger, and Doubt. These emotions are powerful, and if left unchecked, they can take over your mind, making it a place of fear and pain instead of peace and happiness.

The story shows that Love is strong and sometimes has to make hard decisions to protect what's good. Love's greatest enemy is Fear, which tries to use these negative emotions to take control. But by standing up to Fear and being willing to sacrifice these negative feelings, Love can ensure that your mind stays in a place of peace—a personal heaven on earth.

So, the lesson here is clear: to live a happy, peaceful life, you need to protect your mind by letting go of negative emotions, even if it's difficult. By doing so, you allow love and positivity to thrive, creating a better life for yourself and those around you. Our heaven on earth is found in peace and joy. We are precious. We are Love, but we must first discover this Love within ourselves before we can extend it to others. Only when we allow them to, can Negative Emotions and Fear shatter Love. Practice self-love, find contentment, and foster peace to create your heaven on earth.

All emotions are birthed from Love, yet generational traumas tarnish their purity. We must liberate ourselves from this bondage that originated from slavery and reconsider how we perceive and treat each other. Our path to tranquility and joy in this life is consciousness-based and readily accessible to us. Our minds hold the solutions to all conceivable and inconceivable problems. By mastering our emotions, we can shift our outlook and free ourselves from the negative energy that overshadows our lives. Now is the time to find liberation from past traumas and the negative emotions they foster. The past is behind us. The present is a gift, and the future is an opportunity to mold our reality by releasing Fear. Accept that you did the best you could with the resources available at the time. Recognize these experiences as neither good nor bad. Upon reaching this realization, you can begin to live in the present moment and construct a new future.

Will Smith once shared a profound insight about how our emotions shape our responses when we feel cornered. He noted that we all have childhood traumas and experiences that influence our emotions, and as a result, we create characters to represent and defend us in the real world. These characters, crafted by our negative emotions, respond on our behalf when we encounter perplexing situations. When these characters win a few battles for us, we start believing that success is achievable through negative emotional responses. But eventually, these tactics cease to work because these characters are an illusion. They aren't the true you. So, what do you do when you're cornered and these characters you've been masquerading as no longer function in reality? The question then becomes: do you possess the courage? Are you brave enough to eliminate these characters that you've fabricated? Do you have the courage to be yourself? But who exactly are you? Are you the silenced child or the reflective adult?

An African proverb states, "The child who is not embraced by the village will burn it down just to feel its warmth." Disappointment, Sadness, Anger, and Doubt are secondary emotions, mere reflections of a deeper need requiring your attention. My understanding is that all our decisions are driven by either Love or Fear, and even Fear is motivated by the threat of Love's absence. So, always choose Love, unconditionally. Remember, life is a canvas for your imagination. So why not design it to your liking?

We're all Black Boyz, even if your skin bears just a hint of color. Blackness is a source of pride. It's a lifestyle. Being Black allows you to understand Love, Peace, Happiness, and your heaven on earth. Love yourself to mature from Black Boyz to Black Men. Dear Black Men, life is beautiful when we set aside our self-loathing and unite. Remember, The Devil's Perspective is only wrong if seen negatively. With every new perspective you allow into your mind, you discover more about yourself, leading to a more peaceful existence. Change your perspective to change your mindset. With a change in perspective, peace, happiness, and Black excellence will follow.

If you aspire to purchase things without a second glance at the price tag, you must chase your dreams without a second look at the clock. Anyone who advises you to relinquish your dreams doesn't deserve your company. I love you. God loves you. But it means nothing if you don't love yourself. When you fail to love yourself, you'll always yearn for power. Remember to Dream Big, Hustle to Greatness, and Inspire Others Along the Way.

Dear Black Boyz: The Power of Perspectives; I hope you enjoyed it and, most importantly, that it has offered you a fresh perspective.

Final Letter to Black Boyz

Dear Black Boyz,

As I bring this book to a close, I want you to understand something that transcends the pages you've just read, something that reaches into the depths of who you are and pulls forth the greatness that is your birthright. You aren't just Boyz, not just a part of this world—you're the very essence of its future, the seeds of greatness waiting to bloom into the men who'll shape a new reality. Within each of you lies a seed, a seed planted by your ancestors, nourished by the struggles and triumphs of those who came before you. This seed is your potential, your greatness, your higher self. But like any seed, it requires care, attention, and the right conditions to sprout and grow.

The world will try to tell you who you are. It'll try to define you by your skin, by your circumstances, by the limitations it places on you. But I'm here to tell you that the world is wrong. You're not defined by these things. Instead, you're defined by the love you hold within, by the dreams you dare to dream, by the hustle you put into making those dreams a reality, and by the inspiration you share with others along the way.

Love isn't just an emotion; it's your essence. It's the force that connects you to everything and everyone around you. It's the power that makes you unbreakable, the energy that fuels your resilience. When you look in the mirror, I want you to see more than just a reflection of yourself—I want you to see the embodiment of love, the manifestation of all that's good, pure, and true in this world.

Let love be your guide. Let it be the voice that whispers in your ear when you're faced with challenges, when doubt tries to creep into your mind, when fear threatens to paralyze you. Remember that love is stronger than fear, stronger than any negative force that tries to pull you down. When you choose love, you choose life, you choose truth, you choose to rise above.

Dream big, Black Boyz. Your dreams are the blueprints of your future, the visions of what could be if you dare to believe in them. But dreams alone are not enough—you must pair them with action, with hustle, with a relentless pursuit of greatness. Don't let the world shrink your dreams. Don't let anyone tell you that you're dreaming too big. The only limits that exist are the ones you place on yourself.

Your dreams are your gift to the world, the legacy you'll leave behind. They're the proof that you existed, that you mattered, that you lived a life of purpose and passion. So dream, Black Boyz. Dream of the impossible, and then make it possible.

Greatness isn't handed to you; it's earned. It's carved out of the sweat, the struggle, and the sacrifice you put into making your dreams a reality. Hustle is the bridge between your dreams and your accomplishments. It's the fire that keeps you moving forward, even when the path is tough, even when the odds are stacked against you.

There'll be days when you want to give up, when the weight of the world feels too heavy to bear. But remember, Black Boyz, that you come from a long line of warriors, of Kings, of men and women who refused to give up, who fought with everything they had to create a better world for you. Let their strength be your strength, their perseverance be your perseverance. Hustle with all your heart, and know that every step you take brings you closer to your destiny.

As you rise, remember to lift others with you. Your journey isn't just about you—it's also about the impact you have on those around you, the lives you touch, the souls you inspire. Inspiration is the ripple effect of your greatness, the legacy that'll live on long after you're gone. Inspiration is also the byproduct of your dreams and hustle.

Inspire others to dream, to hustle, to love. Show them what's possible when you refuse to settle for anything less than greatness. Be the example, the role model, the light that guides others out of darkness. Your life is a testament to the power of resilience, of hope, of the unwavering belief that you're destined for greatness.

This journey you're on is more than just a path to success; it's a journey of awakening. Awakening to your true self, your higher self—the part of you that's connected to something greater, something divine. This is the self that knows no limits, that fears nothing, that loves unconditionally.

To awaken your higher self, you must first understand that everything you need is already within you. The power, the wisdom, the love—it's all there, waiting for you to tap into it. You aren't lacking; you aren't incomplete. You're whole, you're more than enough, and you're capable of achieving anything you set your mind to.

But this awakening requires courage. It requires the courage to let go of the characters you've created to protect yourself, to strip away the layers of fear, doubt, and insecurity that have been placed on you by the world. It requires the courage to be vulnerable, to be authentic, to be who you truly are.

Dear Black Boyz, the world needs you. It needs your voice, your perspective, your strength. It needs you to be the change that you want to see in the world, to be the leaders, the innovators, the visionaries who'll shape a new reality. You're the answer to the prayers of those who came before you, the manifestation of their hopes and dreams. So stand tall, Black Boyz. Stand in your truth, in your power, in your greatness. Know that you're loved, you're valued, and you're destined for extraordinary things. The seed of greatness is within you—nurture it, protect it, and let it grow into something magnificent.

In every challenge you face, in every obstacle you overcome, remember that you're not alone. You're part of a legacy, a brotherhood, a community of Black Men who've walked this path before you and who walk it with you now. Together, we're unstoppable. Together, we'll create a heaven here on earth.

Wake up!!!
by Relly Rell

Black Boyz Alphabet

A – Achieve
I am destined to achieve greatness, every step I take is towards success.

B – Bold
I am bold in my actions, fearless in pursuit of my dreams.

C – Conquer
I conquer challenges with strength and *determination.*

D – Dream
I dream without limits, and my dreams shape my reality.

E – Elevate
I elevate myself and those around me, rising above all obstacles.

F – Focus
I focus on my goals with clarity and purpose, never wavering.

G – Grow
I grow through every experience, evolving into my best self.

H – Hustle
I hustle with passion, putting in the work to make my dreams come true.

I – Inspire
I inspire others through my actions, leading by example.

J – Justify
I justify my greatness by living a life of purpose and integrity.

K – Know
I know my worth, and I stand firm in my truth.

L – Lead
I lead with courage, guiding myself and others toward success.

M – Master
I master my emotions, energy, and actions, becoming the architect of my destiny.

N – Nourish
I nourish my mind, body, and spirit with positivity and strength.

O – Overcome
I overcome all obstacles with resilience and perseverance.

P – Power
I am power, channeling my energy to create the life I desire.

Q – Quest
I am on a quest for knowledge, self-improvement, and excellence.

R – Rise
I rise above challenges, always reaching for new heights.

S – Strength
I embody strength, both physically and mentally, unshakable in my resolve.

T – Triumph
I triumph over adversity, turning setbacks into comebacks.

U – Ubuntu
I am because we are. I recognize my connection to others and live with compassion and unity.

V – Victory
I claim victory in all my endeavors, knowing that I am destined for greatness.

W – Wisdom
I seek wisdom, learning from every experience to guide my future.

X – Excel
I excel in everything I do, striving for excellence in all areas of my life.

Y – Yes
I say yes to opportunities that align with my vision and values.

Z – Zenith
I reach my zenith, the pinnacle of my potential, through hard work and dedication.

Black Boyz Affirmations

I am Bold: I walk with confidence and face every challenge head-on.

I Dream Big: My dreams are limitless, and I have the power to make them reality.

I Hustle Hard: I work with relentless dedication, knowing that my efforts will pay off.

I Inspire Others: My actions speak louder than words, motivating others to strive for their best.

I Lead with Purpose: I guide my life and others towards success with clarity and vision.

I Live Ubuntu: I understand that my strength comes from the strength of my community, and I uplift those around me.

Black Boyz Code of Conduct

Respect Yourself and Others: Honor your mind, body, and spirit, and extend that respect to those around you.

Speak Life: Use your words to uplift, encourage, and empower. Negative language has no place in your vocabulary.

Take Responsibility: Own your actions, decisions, and outcomes. Accountability is key to growth.

Pursue Excellence: Strive to be your best in all you do. Mediocrity is not an option.

Stay Focused: Keep your eyes on your goals, and don't let distractions derail your path to success.

Uplift Your Community: Live by the principle of Ubuntu; recognize your connection to others and contribute to their well-being.

Embody Integrity: Let your actions reflect honesty, trustworthiness, and moral courage.

Believe in Your Power: Know that you have the strength to overcome any obstacle and achieve greatness.

The Secret to Life for Black Boyz

The secret to life is mastering the energy within you and recognizing the power of your connection to others. By aligning your energy with your dreams, and living by the principles of Ubuntu—understanding that your humanity is tied to the humanity of others—you unlock the full potential of your being. This journey empowers you to create a life of success, peace, and fulfillment, while also uplifting those around you. Embrace your journey, lead with integrity, and never doubt your worth or capabilities. The world is yours for the taking, and together, we rise.

Completion
by Relly Rell

ABOUT THE AUTHOR

Terrell White, known to the world as Relly Rell, has always been conscious of his purpose and destiny—to harness his unique life experiences and insights, and share them with the world. Relly Rell is the alter ego that emerged from Terrell's creative mental landscape, a persona he cultivates and cherishes to this day. Understanding the necessity of a positive perspective, Terrell is committed to influencing the culture with uplifting messages that will resonate with the current and future generations.

As a Black Man who spent his formative years in Lancaster, California, Terrell is intimately aware of the societal conditioning affecting Black Boyz. Armed with an understanding of the mind's power, his mission is now geared towards helping dismantle the mindset of enslavement ingrained in American and European culture. His goal is to facilitate the discovery of peace and joy—terrestrial manifestations of heaven.

Terrell believes that this transformative process starts with recognizing our inherent worth and questioning the conventional knowledge we've been fed. Cultivating an independent mindset, approached through a fresh perspective, is fundamental to this journey. His creatively crafted narratives serve as positive catalysts that challenge entrenched mindsets, instilling new perspectives and leaving an indelible impact on the cultural landscape for future generations.

"Dream, Hustle, Inspire" is not merely a motto for Relly Rell, it is the very essence of his life's mission.

ENDNOTES
WHO ARE YOU?
DREAMS DO COME TRUE

Introducing: Breaking the Chain: Solo Challenge

WHAT IS IT?
"Breaking the Chain: Solo Challenge" is a self-reflective game designed to help you recognize and transform negative thoughts and words into positive, empowering statements. This game is about personal growth, positivity, and embracing the power of unconditional love.

WHY PLAY?
In a world where negativity can often take center stage, "Breaking the Chain" challenges you to shift your mindset. It's more than just a game—it's a journey toward becoming your Higher Self. You'll learn to see greatness in yourself and others, fostering an environment of positivity and love.

HOW TO PLAY:
Spot the Chain (Negative Language):
Observe Yourself: As you go through your day, keep an ear out for any negative thoughts or words you might use, like "I can't" or "I don't know." These are the chains you need to break.
Observe Others: Listen to what the people around you are saying. If you hear someone using negative language, mentally note it as a chain to break.

BREAK THE CHAIN:

Your Thoughts: When you catch yourself thinking or speaking negatively, immediately flip it into something positive. For example, instead of saying "I can't do this," say "I'm capable of finding a way."

Others' Words: When you hear someone else being negative, rephrase it in your mind to something positive. If it feels right, share the positive rephrase with them, but remember—you're not here to judge. Your job is to be the change you want to see in the world.

SCORING:

Negative Thoughts: If you think or say something negative, subtract 2 points.
Positive Rephrasing: If you successfully turn a negative into a positive in your head, add 1 point.
Listening for Negativity: Each time you catch and mentally rephrase someone else's negative words, add 1 point.

END OF DAY REFLECTION:

Add up your points at the end of the day. If you reach +10, you've moved closer to your Higher Self, where positivity is your natural state. If you reach -10, take time to reset by reading Dear Black Boyz and reflecting on its empowering messages.

SUPERPOWER WARNING:

As you continue to play, you'll develop the ability to hear and recognize negativity in yourself and others. But remember—no matter how much negativity you encounter, it's not your job to judge. Your mission is to embody the change you want to see, to see greatness in yourself and everyone around you. In the end, unconditional love is all that matters.

WHY IT MATTERS:

"Breaking the Chain" isn't just about scoring points; it's about becoming a better version of yourself. It's about learning to lead with love, understanding, and positivity. When you can see the best in yourself, you can start seeing it in others, creating a ripple effect of positive change in the world.

So, are you ready to break the chains and step into your Higher Self? Let's play.

NEGATIVE WORDS LIST (CHAINS TO BREAK):

I can't. I don't know. I believe (when it implies doubt). I want. I need. I guess. I'm trying. Okay (when it means settling for less). I'm sick. I hate. I think (when it implies uncertainty). I'm not sure. Any negative speech or self-talk.

☥☥♀ D⊕D ☥☥⊌ SEE 1001

HINT: look in the margins

61 | Dear Black Boyz,

YOU ARE MORE POWERFUL THAN YOU BELIEVE!

10|10

Mirror Mirror Mirror
by Relly Rell

www.ingramcontent.com/pod-product-compliance
Lightning Source LLC
Chambersburg PA
CBHW022123040426
42450CB00006B/822